HOW *to* USE

the Internet

2001 Edition

SAMS

201 West 103rd Street
Indianapolis, Indiana 46290

Rogers Cadenhead

Visually in Full Color

How to Use the Internet

2001 EDITION

International Standard Book Number: 0-672-32000-2

Library of Congress Catalog Card Number: 11-105610

Printed in the United States of America

First Printing: August 2000

02   01   00   4   3   2

Acquisitions Editors
Randi Roger
Jeff Schultz

Development Editors
Damon Jordan
Alice Martina Smith

Managing Editor
Charlotte Clapp

Project Editor
Carol Bowers

Copy Editor
Gene Redding

Indexers
Sandra Henselmeier
Eric Schroeder
Christine Nelsen

Proofreaders
Katherin Bidwell
Mary Ellen Stephenson

Technical Editor
Galen A. Grimes

Technical Assistant
Sunil Hazari

Interior Designer
Nathan Clement

Cover Designers
Nathan Clement
Aren Howell

Layout Technicians
Stacey DeRome
Eric Miller
Tim Osborn
Mark Walchle

Contents at a Glance

Contents

About the Author

Rogers Cadenhead is a writer and Web publisher who has written eight books on Internet-related topics, including *Sams Teach Yourself Java 2 in 21 Days* and *Sams Teach Yourself Microsoft FrontPage 2000 in 24 Hours* but not *Teach Yourself to Be Less Specific in Exactly 1,440 Minutes*. Cadenhead is the author of a trivia column for the *Fort Worth Star-Telegram* and Knight-Ridder News Service and the publisher of the Web sites Cruel Site of the Day (www.cruel.com) and the Drudge Retort (www.drudge.com). Actively involved in computers since childhood, Cadenhead invented the BBS door game in 1982 and left the field without realizing that more than 500,000 of these games would be sold to BBS operators during the next 15 years. To contact the author about this book, visit the World Wide Web site **http://www. prefect.com/internet**

Acknowledgements

Word to all my party peeps at Macmillan Computer Publishing, including **Mark Taber**, **Scott Meyers**, **Randi Roger**, **Alice Martina Smith**, **Gene Redding**, and **Carol Bowers**. They made this book da bomb and are poptastic jiggy and phat dope fresh.

A big shout out to **David and Sherri Rogelberg** of Studio B for representin' when someone temporarily misplaced my props. Wassup!

I also must thank my fly spouse **M.C.** and my bomb diggety sons **Max** and **Eli**. Check it. You bring mad love to the crib, and I have it on good authority that you are both money and all that.

Peace out.

Dedication

*With much love to the **McMinimys**: **Aunt Kay**, **Uncle Rick**, and cousins **Craig**, **Amy**, and **Brent**. Mary and I fondly remember the times in college when we babysat for your family and gorged ourselves on all the edible food in your home. I don't think Craig had ever seen someone eat that many Nutter Butters in one sitting before. Please accept this heartfelt dedication and our warmest regards in lieu of any form of financial compensation.*

Tell Us What You Think!

As the reader of this book, you are our most important critic and commentator. We value your opinion and want to know what we're doing right, what we could do better, what areas you'd like to see us publish in, and any other words of wisdom you're willing to pass our way.

You can fax, email, or write me directly to let me know what you did or didn't like about this book— as well as what we can do to make our books stronger.

Please note that I cannot help you with technical problems related to the topic of this book, and that due to the high volume of mail I receive, I might not be able to reply to every message.

When you write, please be sure to include this book's title and author, as well as your name and phone or fax number. I will carefully review your comments and share them with the author and editors who worked on the book.

Fax: 317-581-4770

Email: `internet_sams@mcp.com`

Mail: Mark Taber
Associate Publisher
Sams Publishing
201 West 103rd Street
Indianapolis, IN 46290 USA

How To Use This Book

The Complete Visual Reference

Each part of this book is made up of a series of short, instructional tasks, designed to help you understand all the information that you need to get the most out of your computer hardware and software.

Click: Click the left mouse button once.

Double-click: Click the left mouse button twice in rapid succession.

Right-click: Click the right mouse button once.

Pointer Arrow: Highlights an item on the screen you need to point to or focus on in the step or task.

Selection: Highlights the area onscreen discussed in the step or task.

Click and Type: Click once where indicated and begin typing to enter your text or data.

Click & Drag

Release

How to Drag: Point to the starting place or object. Hold down the mouse button (right or left per instructions), move the mouse to the new location, and then release the button.

Key icons: Clearly indicate which key combinations to use.

Each task includes a series of easy-to-understand steps designed to guide you through the procedure.

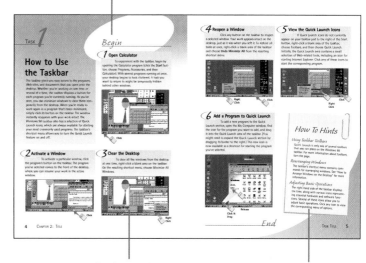

Each step is fully illustrated to show you how it looks onscreen.

Extra hints that tell you how to accomplish a goal are provided in most tasks.

Menus and items you click are shown in **bold**. Information you type is in a `special font`.

Continues

If you see this symbol, it means the task you're in continues on the next page.

Introduction

If you know someone who's into computers, or if you've glanced in the direction of a newspaper or magazine in the last few years, you have probably heard many great things about what the Internet can be used for, including:

✓ Sending and receiving electronic mail

✓ Surfing the World Wide Web

✓ Shopping online

✓ Talking in a chat room

✓ Sending messages with ICQ

✓ Playing MP3 music

You've got a computer that can handle each of these things and a thousand other useful and fun features of the Internet. What you don't have, though, is time to learn all this stuff. Reasons *not* to use the Internet easily come to mind:

Computers are complicated. Software takes hard work to figure out. No one can get hooked up to the Internet without years of diligent study or the help of a teenager. It's like the VCR clock problem all over again—wading through a confusing instruction manual is far worse than looking at a light that blinks 12:00 *over and over for the next 15 or 20 years.*

Right?

Put those thoughts out of your head. *How to Use the Internet* shows how quickly you can get connected and make use of the Internet's most popular services. Whether you're a computer novice or a longtime veteran, the visual, step-by-step instructions in this book show you exactly how to use the Internet on your computer. Pictures show what you see at each step and what you should do with your keyboard and mouse to accomplish a task.

The *How to Use* series of books is for people who want to accomplish specific things without spending time figuring out technical jargon and other computer gobbledygook. In plain English, *How to Use the Internet* answers each of these questions and 100 more:

✓ How to choose an Internet provider

✓ How to connect to the Internet

✓ How to set up Internet Explorer 5

✓ How to revisit your favorite Web pages

✓ How to find a company on the Web

✓ How to send an email message

✓ How to send an attached file

✓ How to buy a product over the Web

You can read this book cover to cover, or you can use it to look up something when you're ready to try it out. Want to hook up ICQ and keep in touch with family members out of state? Turn to Part 8, "Chatting Using Instant Messages with ICQ." Ready to do a little job hunting in one of the Usenet discussion areas you heard about on the news? Turn to Part 7, Task 2, "How to Read a Newsgroup."

How to Use the Internet focuses on the information you need to get going. Most tasks are broken down into seven or fewer steps so that you can get something done right away. When you need to know a little extra, the How-To Hints provide tips that make your Internet experience more complete.

Most of the software you use in this book is on your computer already or can be installed from a CD-ROM that came with your Windows 98 operating system. Any other software you need can be set up at no cost using the Internet—we'll show you how to do that, too.

The only software you need to get started is Windows 98 and the World Wide Web browser that comes with the operating system—Internet Explorer 4 or higher.

How to Use the Internet is the instruction manual for everything you've wanted to do on the Internet.

Computers aren't so complicated. Forget those years of study—I'd rather golf. Any teenager who owes me a favor can tend the garden—there are weeds out there big enough to have their own zip code!

As for your VCR clock, sorry. Ours has been blinking 12:00 since the Carter years.

Task

1

Getting Connected for the First Time

*E*very day, millions of people make use of a worldwide network of computers called the Internet. This network, once the province of scholars, students, and the military, has changed the way many of us communicate, shop, work, and play.

As we embark on a new century, the Internet has quickly made possible concepts that seemed like fanciful science fiction only a few years ago. Students at a Cuernavaca, Mexico, school operate robots housed in a Livermore, California, research lab. A grandmother in Houston sees her newest grandchild for the first time over a video link to her son's home in Indianapolis. A business professor in Iowa sells thousands of books to customers as far away as New Zealand from a spare room in his house.

Windows includes software to connect to the Internet and its most popular services. One of these services is the World Wide Web—millions of documents housed on computers around the world that are linked together to present information as text, graphics, sound, and video. Exploring the Web requires software called a *Web browser*, and one of the most popular is installed along with Windows: Microsoft Internet Explorer.

Before you can use the Web or any other Internet service, you must make a connection between your computer and the Internet. That connection will be used automatically by each program designed to send and receive information using the Internet, such as a Web browser or an email program.

How to Choose an Internet Service Provider

Before you can connect to the Internet, you must have an account with an Internet service provider (ISP). An ISP offers access to the Internet through your computer's modem and can help you set things up when you subscribe. If you don't yet have a service provider, Windows offers several you can choose from. To set up an account with an ISP, you need a credit card; the cost ranges from $9.95 to $29.95 a month. The cheaper rates usually limit the number of hours you can use the Internet and bill you for each additional hour.

Begin

1 Open the Online Services Folder

Double-click the **Online Services** folder on your Windows 98 desktop to open the folder. This folder contains icons for several companies that offer Internet access: AOL, AT&T WorldNet, and others.

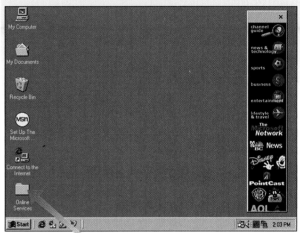

Double-click

2 Choose an Internet Provider

Double-click the icon of a service you'd like to consider. If you double-click the **AT&T WorldNet** icon, for example, a Web page opens that describes the service and gives you a chance to sign up. If you decide to join that ISP, you can use the company's sign-up software to set up your account immediately.

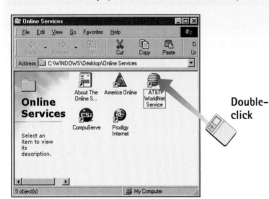

Double-click

3 Set Up Your Internet Provider

Each Internet service has software that must be installed before you can sign up. For example, if you are going to join AT&T WorldNet, click the **OK** button to install it on your system.

Click

4 Choose Your Access Number

From the list of numbers the software provides, pick the *access number* (the number your modem will dial to connect you to the Internet) that's closest to you and that matches the speed of your modem. If you don't know your modem's speed, choose 33,600—the most common speed in use today. After you have entered your billing information, the Internet service is added to the Programs folder of your Start menu (and perhaps to your Windows desktop also).

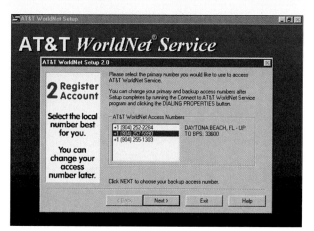

5 Connect to the Internet

From the **Start** menu, select the **Programs** folder. There may be an icon for your Internet service on this menu, or it may be in a folder of its own. Click your service's icon to connect to the Internet through your new service provider.

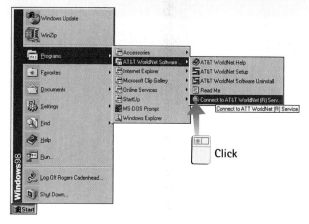

End

How-To Hints

Using the Microsoft Network

You can use Windows to sign up for Microsoft's own Internet service provider: the Microsoft Network. To begin, double-click the **Set Up the Microsoft Network** icon on your Windows desktop.

Finding Other Internet Providers

The companies you can sign up with using Windows are national services, so they may not have a local access number in your area. You can run up sizeable phone bills connecting to the Internet through a long-distance number, so finding an ISP with a local access number is important. You can find local Internet providers in most Yellow Pages under "Internet" or "Internet Services."

How to Set Up an Internet Connection

Most cities, suburbs, and large towns today have local companies that offer Internet service. To find them, look in the Yellow Pages under "Internet" or "Internet Services." These companies often offer a local access number to call, which isn't always available from a nationwide service. You can manually set up an Internet connection to use one of these local companies or any Internet provider.

Begin

1 Open the My Computer Folder

Double-click the **My Computer** icon on your desktop. A folder opens that contains a list of your computer's disk drives, CD-ROM drives, printer connections, and modem connections.

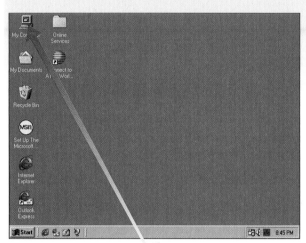

Double-click

2 View Existing Connections

Double-click the **Dial-Up Networking** folder to open a window that displays icons for all the Internet connections that have been set up on your computer. If you have set up an AT&T WorldNet account, you'll see an icon for that service. If you have never used the Internet before, there may not be any connections to see.

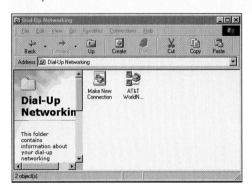

3 Create a New Connection

To create a new connection, you need three things from your Internet service provider (which you located in Task 1): a username, a password, and an access number (telephone number). Double-click the **Make New Connection** icon to create a new Internet connection. The first screen of the **Make New Connection** dialog box opens.

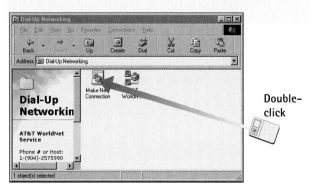

Double-click

4 Name the Connection

The first step is to give the new connection a descriptive name and choose the modem you will use (most computers have only one modem). The name *Local Internet Service* was used in this example. Click **Next** to advance to the next screen of the dialog box.

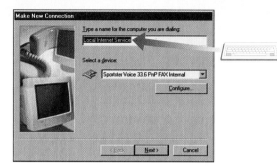

5 Enter Your Provider's Number

Your Internet service provider should have given you the phone number you need to connect to the Internet. For some providers, the access number changes according to the speed of your modem. Enter the access number you were given and select the country from which you're calling. Click **Next** to continue; when Windows says that you have successfully completed the creation of a new connection, click **Finish**.

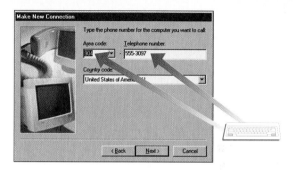

6 Connect to the Internet

A new connection is added to the Dial-Up Networking folder. Double-click this icon to display the **Connect To** dialog box. Type your username and password; select the **Save password** option if you want to avoid typing your password every time you want to use the Internet. Click **Connect** to dial the access number displayed in the dialog box.

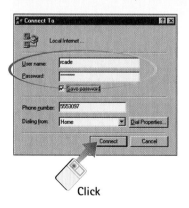

Click

7 Disconnect from the Internet

After you have connected to the Internet, a connection icon appears in the *status area*—the part of your Windows taskbar that's next to the current time. To disconnect from the Internet, double-click this icon; when the **Connected** dialog box opens, click the **Disconnect** button.

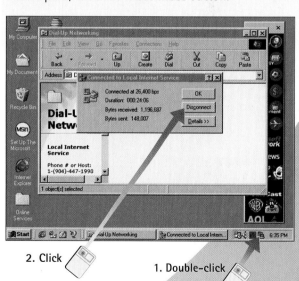

2. Click

1. Double-click

End

How to Connect to the Internet

Before you can surf the World Wide Web or check your email, you must make a connection between your computer and the Internet. Some programs such as Microsoft Internet Explorer will try to connect to the Internet when you begin using them. Other programs will display an error message if you haven't connected first. This task explains what to do when you see the instruction to "connect to the Internet."

Begin

1 List Your Internet Connections

To see what Internet connections are available on your computer, double-click the **My Computer** icon on the desktop; double-click the **Dial-Up Networking** folder to open a list of connection icons.

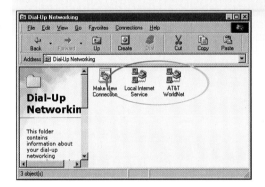

2 Dial Your Access Number

Double-click the icon of the Internet connection you want to use. The **Connect To** dialog box opens. Make sure that your username, password, access number, and dialing location are all correct. Click the **Connect** button to make a connection.

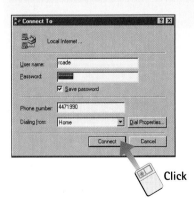

Click

3 Connect to the Internet

If your computer can't connect because of a busy signal or another problem, you'll get the chance to try again or to adjust your Internet settings. The first time you successfully connect, a **Connection Established** window appears.

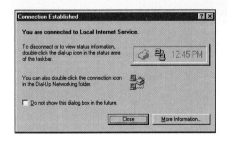

4 Check Your Connection Speed

While you're connected, a connection icon appears on your Windows taskbar near the current time. Double-click this icon to open the **Connected** dialog box; check the speed of your connection. In this example, the speed is 28,800 baud.

Double-click

5 Disconnect from the Internet

When you're ready to disconnect, double-click the connection icon on the Windows taskbar. When the **Connected** dialog box opens, click the **Disconnect** button.

Click

End

How-To Hints

Closing the Connection Established Window

Click the **close** box (the × in the upper-right corner of the dialog box) to shut down the **Connection Established** window while staying connected to the Internet.

How to Connect to the Internet Through a Proxy Server

If you're using the Internet at work, you may not be able to connect directly to the Internet with your Web browser. For security reasons, a *proxy server* is sometimes used as an intermediary between your computer and the Internet. These servers are also called *firewalls*; they make it much more difficult for outsiders to access your computer system or your company's files illegally over the Internet. You can set up Internet Explorer to connect through a proxy server when loading Web pages. This task shows how to set up the server with Internet Explorer 4, the version of the Web browser included with Windows 98.

Begin

1 Start Internet Explorer

Before you can set up Internet Explorer to connect to the Internet through a proxy server, you must have the proxy server's address and port number. When you have that information (check with your network administrator), double-click the **Internet Explorer** icon on your desktop. The **Internet Explorer** window opens and displays a default Web page.

Click

2 Set Your Internet Options

From the **View** menu at the top of the **Internet Explorer** window, select **Internet Options**. The **Internet Options** dialog box opens; you can use this dialog box to customize Internet Explorer.

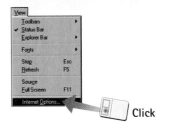

Click

3 Configure Your Connection

Click the **Connection** tab to bring all the settings related to your Internet connection to the front. This window shows how your browser connects to the Internet.

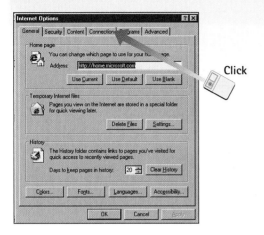

Click

4 Set Up a Proxy Server

Select the **Access the Internet using a proxy server** option and type the address and port number of the server. (This information should have been provided for you by a computer administrator at the place you're accessing the Internet.)

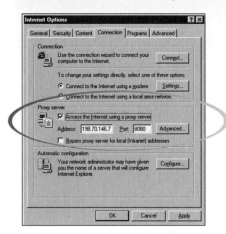

5 Save the New Settings

Click the **OK** button to save your new settings for Internet Explorer and close the dialog box. (The **Apply** button also saves your settings, but it doesn't close the dialog box.) After you save the settings, all attempts to connect to Web pages with your browser will now be routed through the proxy server.

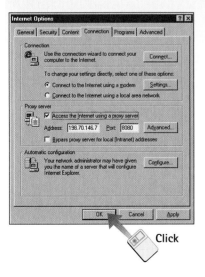

Click

How-To Hints

Bypassing the Proxy Server on an Intranet

If you're using a proxy server in a corporate setting, you might not need it when you're visiting Web pages on your company's intranet. On the **Connection** tab of the **Internet Options** dialog box, select the **Bypass proxy server for local (intranet) addresses** option.

End

How to Load a Web Page

After you connect to the Internet, you are ready to use Internet Explorer, the World Wide Web browsing software included with Windows. If you're not already connected to the Internet when you run Internet Explorer, Windows gives you an opportunity to make a connection.

Begin

_1_ Run Internet Explorer

Double-click the **Internet Explorer** icon on your Windows desktop to run the browser and open a Web page. This starting page is called the browser's _home page_, and it can be set to any page on the Internet or your own computer.

Click

_2_ Explore the Browser

The Internet Explorer window includes a menu bar, toolbar buttons along the top edge of the window, and an Address bar. You'll use all three as you visit different World Wide Web sites. Click the **Search** button in the toolbar at the top of the screen to open a window from which you can search the Web.

Menu bar   Toolbar   Address bar

Click

How-To Hints

Returning to Your Browser's Home Page

The first page your Web browser displays when you open the program is its _home page_. Click the browser's **Home** button (usually in the toolbar at the top of the window) at any time to return to this page.

3 Search the Web

Internet Explorer works with several different *search engines*—sites that catalog millions of Web pages and enable you to search for specific text. Enter the text you want to look for and click the button or graphic that begins the search.

Click

4 View Search Results

The results of your search are presented as a list of Web page titles. Each of these is a *hyperlink*—text or a graphic you can click to load a new page in your browser. Click one of these hyperlinks to go to the linked page.

5 Load a Web Page

The Web page associated with the hyperlink is loaded in the window to the right of the search results list. Click the **Search** button along the top of the Internet Explorer window to close the search results page.

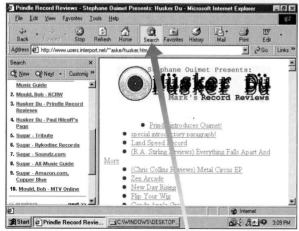

Click

6 View a Page's Address

Every Web page has a unique address called a URL—short for uniform resource locator—which is displayed in the Address bar at the top of the Internet Explorer window. You can type URLs into the Address bar to load pages in the browser. Type **http://www.yahoo.com** in the bar and press **Enter** to visit the Yahoo! Web site.

End

How to Download Internet Explorer 5

Although Internet Explorer is a standard part of Windows, Microsoft has released a new version of its Web browser that you can use with any Windows operating system. Internet Explorer 5 includes new features for faster Web searches, typo correction, Internet radio stations, and content filtering. There also are enhancements to how fast Web pages are displayed and for increased support of new standards of page design. You can download and install this program using your current Web browser.

Begin

1 Visit the Internet Explorer Site

Start Internet Explorer. Type `http://www.microsoft.com/windows/ie/` in the Address bar and press **Enter**. You are taken to your operating system's Internet Explorer home page.

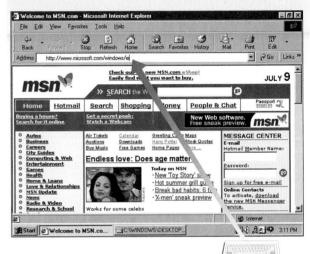

2 View Files You Can Download

Click the **Download Now** link on the Internet Explorer home page. You'll see a page describing the version of Internet Explorer that is right for your computer.

Click

3 Download Internet Explorer 5

When you click **Download Now** on the first page, the Windows Update chooses the appropriate version of Internet Explorer 5 for your computer. Simply click **Download Now** on this page, too, and the process will begin.

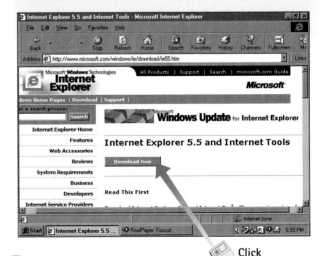

Click

4 Download Internet Explorer 5

After clicking Download Now, you'll see a dialog box asking whether to save Internet Explorer 5's installation program on your system. Choose the **Save this program to disk** option and click **OK**. The **Save As** dialog box opens.

Click

5 Save the Program

Click the down arrow next to the **Save in** field and select the **My Documents** folder. Click the **Save** button to choose this as the place where Internet Explorer's installation program will be saved.

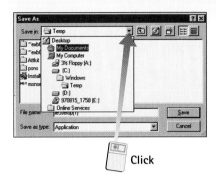

Click

End

How to Set Up Internet Explorer 5

The current version of Internet Explorer 5 is available from Microsoft's Web site, along with Internet Tools software such as Outlook Express and the Windows Media Player. After you have downloaded the setup program (as described in Task 6), you can run the setup program to download and install Internet Explorer 5 and Internet Tools.

Begin

1 Begin the Installation

To begin setting up Internet Explorer 5, close all other programs and connect to the Internet. Open the folder where the installation program is stored—**My Documents** if you completed Task 6—and double-click the **ie5setup** icon. The **Windows Update** dialog box opens.

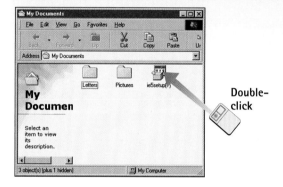

Double-click

2 Choose What to Install

The size of the file you will download depends on whether you want enhancements such as Outlook Express and the Windows Media Player. To install everything, click the radio button next to **Install Now - Typical set of components**, and then click the **Next** button.

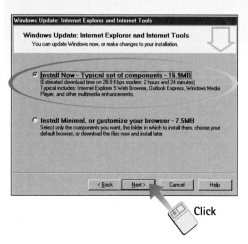

Click

3 Select a Download Site

Microsoft may give you a choice of sites from which you can download installation files. Pick the one closest to your location in the **Download Sites** list and then click the **Next** button.

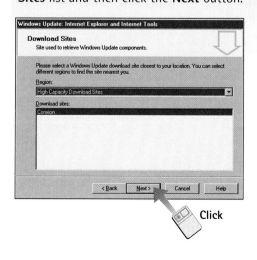

Click

4 Resume an Interrupted Setup

A dialog box appears if the download is interrupted for any reason. Click the **OK** button to close this box. To resume the setup where you left off, connect to the Internet and repeat Step 1.

Click

5 Complete the Download

After all files have been downloaded, the computer must reboot to complete the installation. Close all other programs you're running; when you're ready to restart the computer, click the **Finish** button.

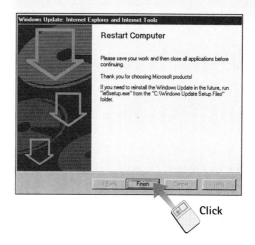

Click

6 Run Internet Explorer 5

After your system has rebooted, run Internet Explorer 5 by double-clicking the **Internet Explorer** icon on your desktop.

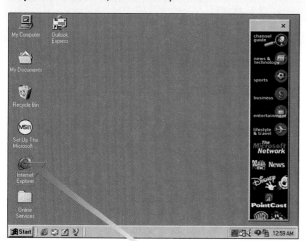

Double-click

End

Task

2

Browsing the World Wide Web

Although the Internet dates back to 1969, for most of its first three decades, the network was the province of scholars, students, and the U.S. military. It was largely a research tool for the academic community and required above-average technical skills to use.

This changed with the popularization of a new Internet information service called the World Wide Web. The Web, which was invented by Tim Berners-Lee of the European Laboratory for Particle Physics in 1989, was designed to be an easy way to publish and share information. It also became the easiest way for millions of people to receive information over the Internet.

The World Wide Web uses *hypertext*—a way of publishing information so that documents can be linked to relevant places in other documents. Using a link takes you to the associated document; it's a way to quickly find and make use of information stored on a variety of computers around the world. Everything that's on the Web can be connected together, creating the largest database of knowledge in human history.

A *Web browser* such as Internet Explorer 5 enables you to visit sites on the Web and view the information contained on those sites' pages, whether it is presented as text, graphics, video, audio, or some other format. ●

How to Use a Web Site

The easiest way to navigate the World Wide Web is to use *hyperlinks*—text or images on a Web page that can be clicked to load another document in your browser. Hyperlinks can connect to anything on the Web, such as pages, graphics files, and programs you can download. Internet Explorer 5 has a toolbar with useful buttons you can use as you're visiting Web pages. Most of the time, as you move from one Web page to another, you use hyperlinks to move.

Begin

1 Load Internet Explorer

The first Web page loaded by Internet Explorer is its *home page*—often a page on the Microsoft Network or one hosted by your computer's manufacturer. Click the **Home** button in Internet Explorer to go to your browser's home page.

Click

2 Click a Hyperlink

Web pages often contain hyperlinks that make it easy to visit other pages. Your mouse pointer changes to a hand when it's over a hyperlink. Click a hyperlink to load the Web page or other document associated with the link.

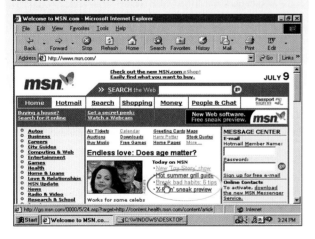

3 Go Back to the Last Page

If you have viewed several Web pages, you can click the **Back** button on the Internet Explorer toolbar to return to the previous page that was displayed in your browser.

 Click

4 Move Forward Again

After you have used the **Back** button, you can click the **Forward** button on the toolbar to see the page you displayed after the current one. **Back** and **Forward** can cycle through all the pages you've looked at while Internet Explorer has been running.

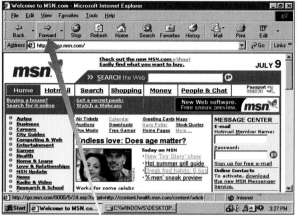

 Click

5 Reload the Current Page

Click the toolbar's **Refresh** button to reload the current page. When Web pages are updated constantly, you can use **Refresh** to make sure that you are viewing the most current version of a page.

Click

6 Stop Loading a Page

If you decide not to wait for a Web page to finish loading, click the **Stop** button. Your Web browser displays everything that was loaded up to that point, as if it were the entire document.

 Click

How-To Hints

Opening Pages in a New Window

Internet Explorer can open Web pages in a new window, leaving the current page on display. Right-click a hyperlink and select the **Open a New Window** command from the context menu.

End

How to Visit a Web Site When You Know Its Address

Everything you can display on the World Wide Web has a unique address called a URL, which stands for *uniform resource locator*. Internet Explorer 5's Address bar normally shows the URL of the document currently being displayed. One exception: Some Web sites display their primary URLs even if you load a different page. If you know a Web page's URL, you can get there without using hyperlinks.

Begin

1 Display the Address Bar

The **Address bar** displays the current URL, and it also can be used to load a different Web page using its URL. If it is not visible, double-click the **Address** label in the bar at the top of the Internet Explorer window. The bar expands to show an Address combo box.

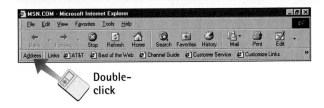

Double-click

2 Enter a URL

To go directly to a Web page, type its URL in the Address bar and press **Enter**. Internet Explorer attempts to load the document associated with that URL, if one exists. Try this by typing **http://www.yahoo.com** in the Address bar and pressing **Enter**.

3 Use a Shortcut

Internet Explorer can find many popular Web sites even if you only know a site's name or its subject matter. To see this in action, type **Excel** in the Address bar and press **Enter**. The browser's Autosearch feature looks for a URL that best matches the topic keyword *Excel*.

4 Find the Best Site

If Autosearch can match a URL with the topic, that URL is loaded by the browser. A search pane also appears in the lower-left corner of the window, which lists other sites you may be looking for. Click the close button to close that window.

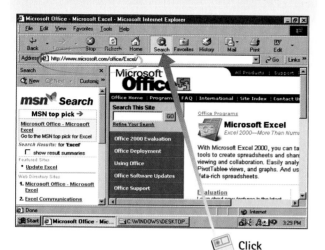

Click

5 Select an Address Again

Click the arrow next to the Address bar to see a list of entries you have recently typed into the bar, including URLs and Autosearch shortcuts. Click an item in the list to enter it into the Address bar again and to load the page or Autosearch pane in the browser window.

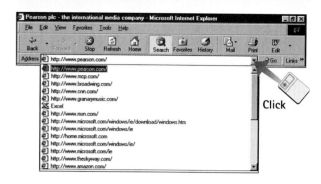

Click

6 Remove Address Bar Requests

Internet Explorer automatically deletes past Address bar requests after a designated number of days. You also can delete all the entries manually. Pull down the **Tools** menu and choose **Internet Options**. The **Internet Options** dialog box opens.

Click

7 Clear the History Folder

Address bar requests are stored in Internet Explorer's **History** folder. Click the **Clear History** button to delete all the entries from the **History** folder *and* the Address bar drop-down list.

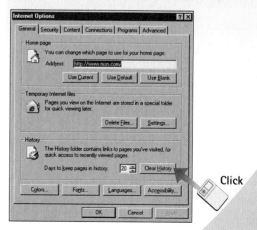

Click

End

How to Revisit Your Favorite Web Pages

One of the biggest timesavers Internet Explorer 5 provides is the Favorites list, which holds shortcuts to Web pages you visit frequently. Internet Explorer comes with a default list of favorites when it is installed (this list often has been customized by your computer manufacturer). You can easily edit the Favorites list by adding and removing your own shortcuts. The Favorites list is organized like a file folder in Windows Explorer.

Begin

1 Visit Your Favorite Sites

In Internet Explorer, click the **Favorites** button to open the Favorites list. The list is organized like a file folder, and it can contain both Internet shortcuts and subfolders. (Note that you don't have to be connected to the Internet to edit your list of favorites.)

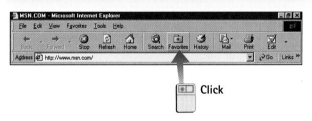

Click

2 Select an Internet Shortcut

To load a Web page from the Favorites list, click its Internet shortcut. If you are not connected to the Internet, the **Connect To** dialog box opens. Click **Connect** to dial your Internet service provider and make a connection.

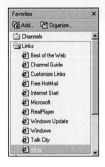

3 Add the Current Site to the List

If you'd like to add the currently displayed Web document to your Favorites list, click the **Add** button.

 Click

4 Save Your New Favorite

You can save the new Internet shortcut in any folder that's part of the Favorites list. Internet Explorer provides a name for the shortcut, which you can change by editing it in the **Name** text box.

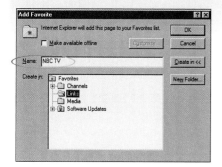

5 Delete a Site from the List

To remove a shortcut from the Favorites list, right-click the item and select **Delete** from the context menu that appears.

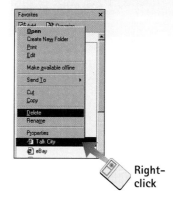

Right-click

6 Move a Site to a New Folder

You can move shortcuts to different folders in the Favorites list. Drag the shortcut from its present location to a new folder; release the mouse button to make the change.

Drag & Drop

End

How-To Hints

Renaming an Internet Shortcut

You can give a shortcut a new name: Right-click the shortcut, select the **Rename** command from the context menu, type the new name, and press **Enter**.

Adding New Favorites Quickly

You can add favorites in Internet Explorer even if the Favorites list is not visible: With the Web document you want to add displayed in the browser, pull down the **Favorites** menu and choose the **Add to Favorites** command. This menu also contains every one of the shortcuts in your list.

How to Load a Web Page for Faster Viewing

Internet Explorer 5 can speed up your use of the World Wide Web considerably by downloading your favorite sites ahead of time. These sites can be viewed while you're *offline*—disconnected from the Internet—and often are much faster to load if you're using a dial-up account to connect to the Internet. You can set up a Web page for offline viewing as you're adding it to your Favorites list.

Begin

1 Select Offline Browsing

To add the page you're viewing to the Favorites list, pull down the **Favorites** menu and choose **Add to Favorites**. In the **Add Favorite** dialog box that appears, choose the folder in which you want to store your new favorite and select the **Make available offline** option. Don't click the **OK** button yet.

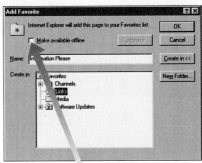

Click

2 Use the Offline Wizard

Click the **Customize** button to start the **Offline Favorite Wizard**, a program that makes it easier to set up a page for offline reading.

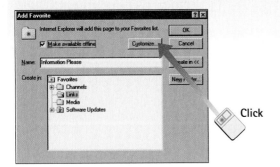
Click

3 Save Linked Pages

You can retrieve pages that are linked to your new favorite, even if they're not part of the same Web site. To save linked pages, click the **Yes** radio button.

4 Choose How Much to Retrieve

Use the **Download pages** text box to specify how many links Internet Explorer should follow as it looks for documents to retrieve. Higher values save more pages for offline browsing, but they also take more time to retrieve. Click the **Next** button to continue.

Click

5 Choose When to Retrieve Pages

You can retrieve a favorite for offline viewing in two ways—manually or at a scheduled time each day. For the latter, click the radio button next to **I would like to create a new schedule**. Click the **Next** button to continue.

6 Set Up a Schedule

Choose the time and days on which pages should be retrieved. There's also an option to connect to the Internet automatically at a scheduled time, if you're not already connected. Click the **Next** button, answer the wizard's remaining questions, and click the **OK** button to add this new Internet shortcut to the Favorites list.

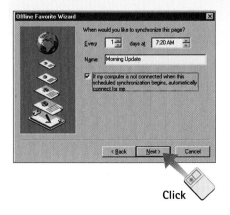

Click

7 Download Offline Pages Manually

To immediately retrieve all pages set up for offline browsing without waiting for a scheduled time, pull down the **Tools** menu, then choose the **Synchronize** command.

Click

End

How to Pick a New Home Page for Your Browser

A term you'll see often on the World Wide Web is *home page*—the main page of a Web site, which usually can be used to reach every section of the site. There's another kind of home page—the one loaded by a Web browser when it first runs. Internet Explorer 5 includes a **Home** button on its main tool-bar, which you can use to quickly return to the browser's home page. You can change this page at any time.

Begin

1 Set Up a New Home Page

Your Internet Explorer home page can be any page on the World Wide Web or even a page stored on your own system. When you have found a page you want to use as the browser's home page, load it with your browser.

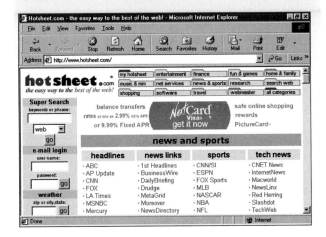

2 Adjust Your Browser Settings

With your prospective home page loaded, pull down the **Tools** menu and choose **Internet Options**. The **Internet Options** dialog box opens, which you use to adjust your browser's Internet settings.

Click

3 Display the General Settings

The **Internet Options** dialog box has six tabs that display different settings you can adjust. If the General tab is hidden behind another tab, click the **General** tab to bring it to the front.

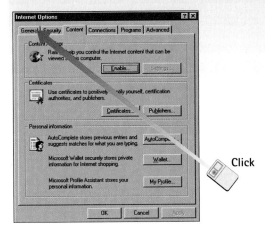

Click

4 Change Your Home Page

The **Address** text box identifies your browser's home page. Click the **Use Current** button to change this to the page currently displayed by your browser. If you decide to restore Internet Explorer's original home page, click the **Use Default** button. To save any changes you've made and exit the dialog box, click the **OK** button.

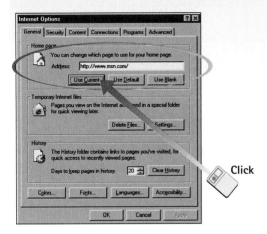

Click

5 Load Your Home Page

Click the **Home** button to return to your browser's home page at any time. When the home page loads in the browser, it will be the new page you just specified.

Click

End

How-To Hints

Using a Blank Home Page

You can make your Internet Explorer home page an empty one that loads faster than the other alternatives. To set this up, choose **Tools, Internet Options**; click the **General** tab in the **Internet Options** dialog box and then click the **Use Blank** button. Click **OK** to exit the dialog box. If you use a blank page as your home page, you can make use of your Favorites list or the Address bar to visit Web pages.

Using a Page Stored on Your Computer

Any page that Internet Explorer can display is suitable for use as the browser's home page. To open a Web page stored on your computer, choose **File, Open**; in the **Open** dialog box, click the **Browse** button to find any document on your system and click **OK** to open it. The document then can be set as your home page using Steps 2 through 5 of this task.

How to Change Internet Explorer's Settings

While using Internet Explorer 5, you can customize the way the browser looks, displays information, and operates. You've already used some of the software's customization features to set up a new home page and clear out past Address bar requests. There are more than 100 other settings you can adjust with the **Internet Options** dialog box, which is accessible from the **Tools** menu.

Begin

1 Configure Your Browser

To get started, pull down the **Tools** menu and choose **Internet Options**. The **Internet Options** dialog box opens.

Click

2 Set Your Internet Options

To see groups of related settings, click the tabs along the top edge of the **Internet Options** dialog box. Click the **General** tab to display some of the browser's main settings.

3 Clean Out Temporary Files

As you use Internet Explorer, Web pages you view are saved along with graphics and other files included on a page. These files are stored in a subfolder called **Temporary Internet Files** in your main **Windows** folder. Your browser eventually deletes these files, but you can do so immediately: Click the **Delete Files** button. You'll be asked to confirm by clicking **OK** before any files are deleted.

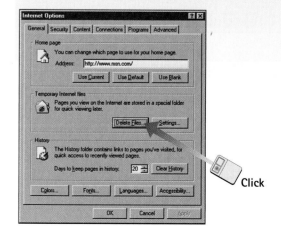

Click

4 Adjust the Size of the History Folder

Internet Explorer deletes temporary files when the folder they are stored in exceeds a maximum size. To adjust this maximum, click the **Settings** button to open the **Settings** dialog box. Drag the **Amount of disk space to use** slider, releasing it where you want the new maximum to be. Click **OK** to confirm and return to the **Internet Options** dialog box.

Drag

5 Change the Default Font

You can make many Web pages more readable by choosing different fonts for the text they display. Click the **Fonts** button on the **General** tab to open the Fonts dialog box. Select a default font for Web pages and a default font for other text. Click **OK** to save your changes.

6 Close the Internet Options Dialog Box

When you have finished changing the settings in the **Internet Options** dialog box, click **OK** to save your settings and close the dialog box. The next time you start your browser, all your new settings will be in effect.

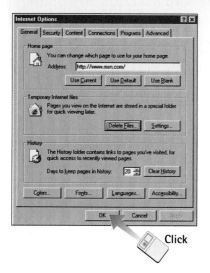

Click

How-To Hints

Making Your Font Selections Take Precedence

Normally, if a Web page is designed to use a specific font, that font is displayed instead of the one you specified for the browser in Step 5. You can change this in the **Internet Options** dialog box: On the **General** tab, click the **Accessibility** button, then select the **Ignore font styles specified on Web pages** option.

End

How to Print a Web Page

Internet Explorer 5, like many Windows programs, offers the capability to print documents. You can print the current Web page as it appears in the browser, print all hyperlinks on a page, and even follow those hyperlinks and print every one of those pages at the same time. Web pages can be displayed on a printer, sent out using a fax modem, and saved as a disk file optimized for printing.

Begin

1 Choose the Print Command

To print the Web page that's currently displayed in the browser window, pull down the **File** menu and choose the **Print** command. The **Print** dialog box opens.

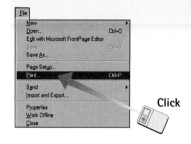

Click

2 Choose a Printer

You can send Web pages to any printer or fax modem that has been installed on your system. To select a printer, click the arrow next to the **Name** drop-down list and drag to select the correct device.

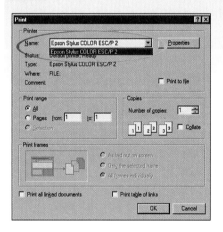

3 Print Associated Web Pages

Internet Explorer also can look at all hyperlinks on the current page and print the pages associated with those links. Select the **Print all linked documents** option at the bottom edge of the **Print** dialog box to print these linked pages.

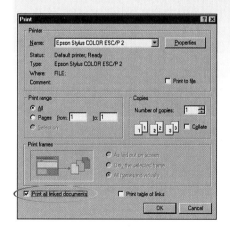

4 List All Hyperlinks

At the same time you print the Web page, you can print a report listing all the page's hyperlinks. Select the **Print tables of links** option to print the list.

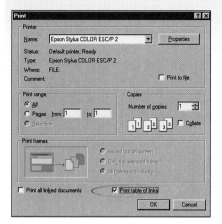

5 Print a Framed Web Page

Some World Wide Web sites divide the browser window into *frames*—separate sections that can have their own scrollbars and borders. You have three options when printing a page that uses frames: print each frame individually, print the page as it looks in the browser, and print only the selected frame. To select a frame, click your mouse in that section of the page before printing the page and then select the **Only the selected frame** option.

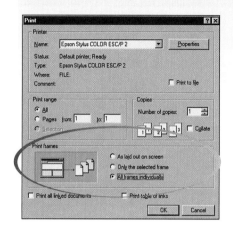

6 Print the Selected Frame

Click the **OK** button to print the Web page according to the options you have selected. Your printer's dialog box opens, displaying the status of the printing operation. You should soon hear the printer working on the page.

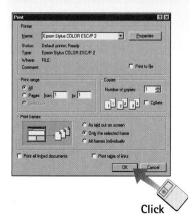

Click

How-To Hints

Making a Page Easier to Print

If you're printing a Web page with a lot of graphics, you may want to make the graphics easier to print by dithering them. *Dithering* simplifies a graphic by reducing the number of colors it contains. In the **Print** dialog box, click the **Properties** button to set your printer's properties. Click the **Graphics** tab to choose a new dithering setting: **None, Coarse, Fine, Line Art**, or **Error Diffusion**. The **Coarse** setting should be sufficient for most purposes when printing a Web page.

End

How to Send a Page to Someone Else Using Email

As you're visiting sites on the World Wide Web, you may run across something that's worth telling a friend or colleague about. Internet Explorer 5 can send hyperlinks and full Web pages using your preferred email program. When you first set up the browser, it is configured to work with Outlook Express, the email program included with Windows. This is easy to change if you use Eudora, Hotmail, or another popular email service. (One program you *can't* use is America Online—its email program is incompatible with this browser feature.)

Begin

1 Mail a Hyperlink

To mail a hyperlink to someone from within Internet Explorer, load the page you want to recommend to someone else, choose **File**, **Send**, **Link by E-mail**. A new message is opened in your preferred email program.

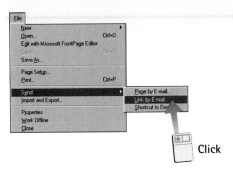

Click

2 Address and Mail the Link

The email message that Internet Explorer created for you includes the hyperlink to the current page in Internet Explorer. You can add comments of your own to go with it. Enter the email address of the recipient in the **To** text box and click **Send** to deliver the message.

Click

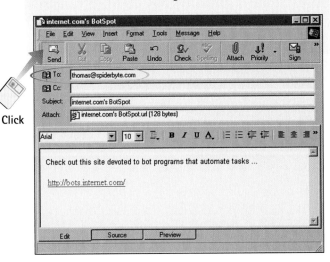

How-To Hints

Configuring Your Email Account

When sending email, Internet Explorer uses the settings that have been established for your email program. If you haven't set up your program to send and receive email, you can learn how to do so in Part 6, "Communicating with Electronic Mail."

Sending a Link to Your Desktop

Another place you can send a hyperlink is to your system's desktop: Choose **File**, **Send**, **Shortcut to Desktop**. An Internet shortcut to the current Web page will be placed on the desktop.

3 Mail a Web Page

To send an entire Web page using email, open the page in Internet Explorer and then choose **File**, **Send**, **Page by E-mail**. A new message is opened in your email program containing a copy of the entire Web page.

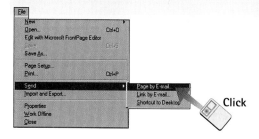

Click

4 Address and Mail the Page

You can make changes to a Web page before emailing it. To send the page, enter the recipient's address in the **To** text box and click the **Send** button.

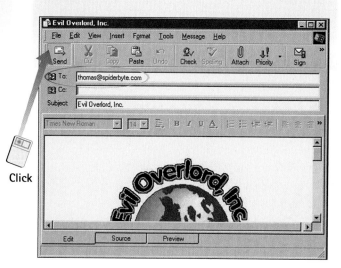

Click

5 Work with a Different Email Program

Internet Explorer is initially set up to work with Outlook Express, an email program included with Windows. To set a different program for email, choose **Tools**, **Internet Options** to open the **Internet Options** dialog box.

Click

6 Select a Program

In the **Internet Options** dialog box, click the **Programs** tab. You'll see six different tasks that Internet Explorer hands off to other programs, including email. Click the arrow next to the **E-mail** pull-down list box and drag down to the email program you want to use. Click **OK** to close the dialog box. The next time you follow the steps in this task, the new email program you specified here is the one that will be used.

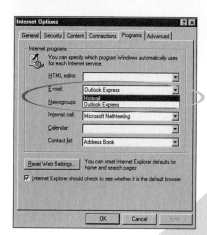

End

How to View Video on a Web Page

Audio and video are becoming more commonplace on the World Wide Web. To view video files on the Web, you must have a video playback program in addition to your browser. Two of the most popular are Microsoft Windows Media Player and the Real Networks RealPlayer. Both of these may have already been installed when you set up Internet Explorer 5.

Begin

1 Install a Video Player

Video files on the Web are loaded like any other document—you click a hyperlink or enter the document's URL in the Address bar. When you are connected to the Internet and you try to open a video file, Internet Explorer checks to see if you have a program that can play the file. If not, a dialog box opens, asking if you want to install a player. To install Windows Media Player, click the **Download** button.

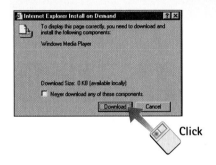

Click

2 Play a Video

The Windows Media Player and RealPlayer programs both have controls that resemble a VCR's buttons—you can play, pause, and stop a video using these controls. Click the **Pause** button to stop playing a video while saving your position; click the **Play** button again to resume playback at the point where you left off.

3 Move to a New Position

Although the Windows Media Player has **Fast Forward** and **Rewind** buttons, there's a quicker way to move to another spot in the video: Drag the playback slider to a new position. This slider moves from left to right to indicate how much of the video has been played.

Drag

4 Adjust the Size of the Display Area

Videos can be displayed at different sizes by dragging the edges of the Windows Media Player window. You also can pick one of three designated sizes by choosing **View, Zoom** and then selecting **50%, 100%,** or **200%.** The larger you expand the size, the more grainy the video will appear.

5 Adjust the Volume

To adjust the video's volume, drag the volume slider to a new position.

Drag

6 Add Closed Captioning

If the video you're playing includes support for closed captioning, you can display this text by choosing **View, Captions.** The Windows Media Player controls are replaced with the **Captions** window. To see the player's controls again, choose **View, Captions** again.

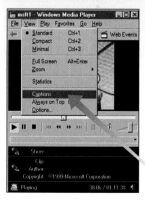

 Click

End

How-To Hints

Playing MP3 Files with Windows Media Player

Windows Media Player supports playback of MP3 audio files, but this feature may not be enabled when you first use the player. Choose **Views, Options**; in the **Options** dialog box, click the **Format** tab. Check the box next to **MP3 File** to enable Windows Media Player to handle these files.

Finding Video Files on the Web

If you're looking for video files to use when trying out Windows Media Player, Microsoft has launched a new site devoted to audio and video presentations on the Web. Visit the Windows Media Web site at **http://windowsmedia.msn.com**.

Task

Visiting a Portal Web Site

When someone begins to use the World Wide Web for the first time, one thing he or she may find surprising is the lack of an official place to start. You can begin exploring the Web at any page, end at any page, and visit any place you like in between.

Although this lack of structure is one of the Web's strong suits, some of the most popular Web sites are designed to be great starting places for your online explorations. These sites are called *portals* because they're intended to be gateways to the huge amount of information that has been amassed on the Web.

Popular portals include Yahoo!, Excite, Netscape, Lycos, Snap!, and the Microsoft Network. The core offering of these portals is a way to find Web sites on specific topics. You can enter keywords and see a list of relevant categories and Web sites.

Portals also offer numerous services to keep you from leaving the site at all—news, sports scores, stock tickers, free email, and dozens of other attractions.

Every one of the major portals offers a way to customize its site to emphasize the topics that interest you most. Many of these services begin with the word *My*, as in *My Yahoo!*, *My Lycos*, and *My Netscape*. ●

How to Set Up an Account on a Portal

For many Internet users, the first World Wide Web site they used as a portal was Yahoo!, a directory of Web sites hand-picked by editors that launched in 1994. This directory, one of the first of its kind, has been one of the Internet's 10 most popular sites for years, attracting millions of visitors each day. Today, the Yahoo! directory of sites is only one of the services it offers. There are also local phone listings, stock prices, free email accounts, and a dozen other features. Yahoo! offers free accounts through the My Yahoo! service.

1 Visit the Portal

Each Web portal has a different procedure for setting up an account, though most require the same things: your name, address, email address, and demographic information such as your profession and household income. To begin setting up a free My Yahoo! account, type **http://my.yahoo.com** into your browser's Address bar and press **Enter**.

2 Request an Account

If you do not have an account, each portal will offer links you can use to request one. On the main My Yahoo! page, there's a **Get Your Own My Yahoo!** hyperlink. Click this link to request an account.

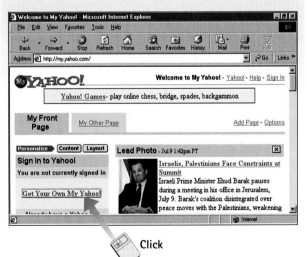

Click

3 Choose a Unique ID

Each portal asks you to choose a unique username, which identifies you throughout the site and forms part of your free email address. In the **Yahoo! ID** text box, type a username that contains only a combination of letters, numbers and underscore characters (_).

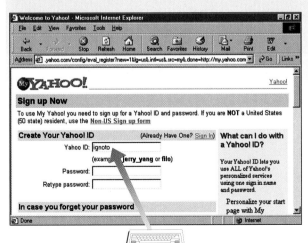

4 Enter Your Email Address

Although portals such as Yahoo! provide free email accounts, you must have an existing email address in order to join Yahoo!, such as the one provided by your Internet service provider. Type this address into the **Current Email Address** text box.

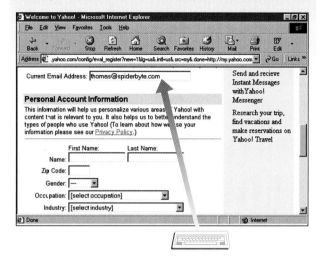

5 Complete the Sign-Up Form

When signing up for a portal, you may be asked several optional questions about your job, interests, and other information. (On My Yahoo!, your real name is even optional.) After you've answered all mandatory questions and any optional ones you choose to provide, click the **Submit this form** button.

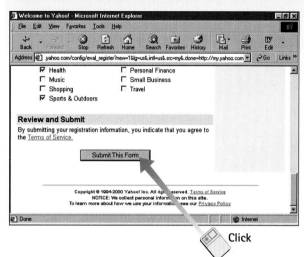

Click

6 Choose an Alternate ID

In most cases, your first choice for a portal username will already be in use by someone else—thousands of people signed up before you did, leaving few common words, names, or surnames up for grabs. Yahoo! suggests a few alternatives to your first choice that are available. You also can try any other usernames until you find one that isn't taken.

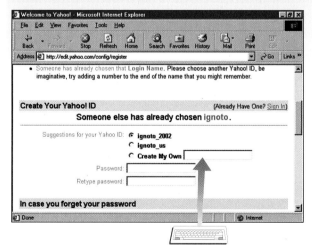

How-To Hints

Trying Other Portal Sites

Yahoo! has comparable offerings to the other large portal sites, so you may want to sign up for several. Visit the following Web sites to set up accounts:

✓ **Excite:** http://www.excite.com

✓ **Go Network:** http://www.go.com

✓ **Microsoft Network:** http://www.msn.com

✓ **My Lycos:** http://my.lycos.com

✓ **My Netscape:** http://my.netscape.com

✓ **My Snap!:** http://www.snap.com

End

How to Personalize a Web Portal

After you have established an account on a portal such as Yahoo!, you can personalize the site to focus on the news, information, and services you are most interested in. For each selected topic, current headlines will be displayed on a page created for your account. You also can add hyperlinks, check local weather and travel information, read your email, and search for Web sites.

Begin

1 Load Your Portal Home Page

After you set up a portal account, your Web browser stores your username and other account settings in a *cookie*, a special browser file stored on your system. Sites can read cookie files they have created, which enables a service such as My Yahoo! to recognize who you are when you visit.

2 Edit a Subject Area

My Yahoo! groups information into topic areas such as television, health, weather, and technology. Many of the subjects have an **Edit** button next to the topic heading. Click a topic's **Edit** button to customize how it is presented.

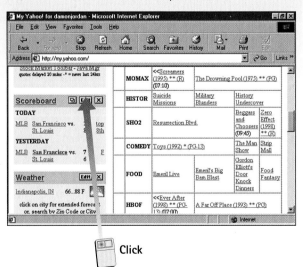

Click

3 Customize a Topic

The Health Tips topic of My Yahoo! can be customized for men, women, parents, and fitness enthusiasts. Click the name of a tip to highlight it, then click the **Add** button to add it to your portal. The **Remove** button does the opposite. Each selected tip will appear on the main My Yahoo! page.

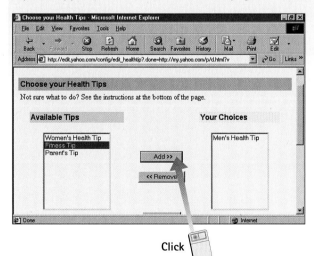

Click

4 Make Your Changes Permanent

Click the **Finished** button to save the changes you've made. Your custom portal page will load using your newly personalized settings.

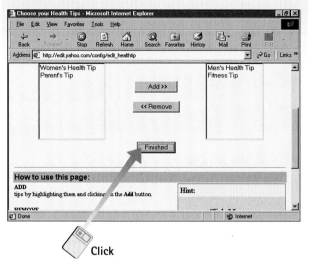

Click

5 Delete a Subject

If you're not interested in a topic on your My Yahoo! page, click the × button adjacent to the topic heading. You'll be asked on another page to confirm the deletion by clicking the **Yes** hyperlink.

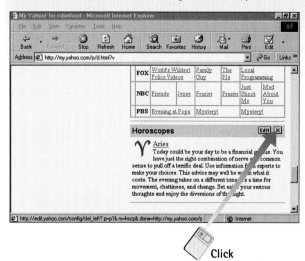

Click

6 Add a Subject

To add subjects to My Yahoo!, scroll down to the **Personalize This Page** heading. Pull down the left or right drop-down menu to the subject you want to add, then click the corresponding **Add** button.

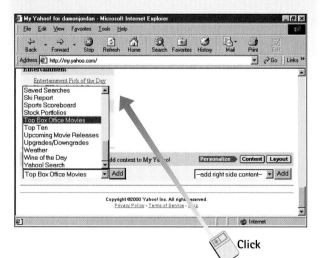

Click

7 Choose New Content

To add or remove multiple topics, click the **Content** button to see a checklist of all available topics. Check the box next to each topic you want to add, and uncheck the boxes of all you want to omit. Click the **Finished** button when you're done.

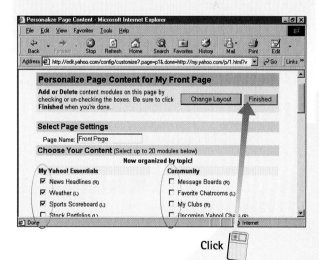

Click

End

How to Make a Portal Your Browser's Home Page

Task 5 in Part 2, "Browsing the World Wide Web," described how to turn any Web page into Internet Explorer 5's home page. The browser's home page appears when it is first run and whenever the **Home** button is clicked, making it a useful starting point for your Web explorations. If you have personalized a Web portal using a service such as My Yahoo!, you might find it useful to make this page your browser's home page.

Begin

1 Visit Your Portal

To get started, load your portal's customized page with your Web browser. For My Yahoo!, type **http://my.yahoo.com** into your Address bar and press **Enter**.

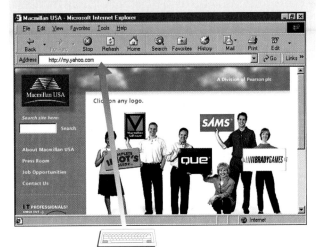

2 Adjust Your Browser Settings

After the page has loaded, pull down the **Tools** menu to the **Internet Options** command to adjust the Internet settings of the browser.

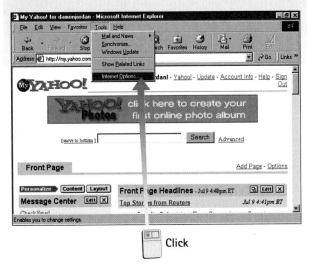

Click

3 Display the General Settings

The six tabs on the **Internet Options** dialog box display different settings you can adjust. Click the **General** tab to bring its settings to the front.

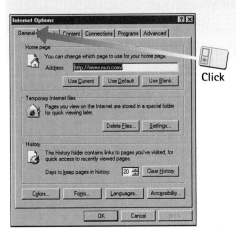

Click

4 Make Your Portal the Home Page

The current home page used by your browser is displayed in the **Address** text box. Click the **Use Current** button to change this to the customized portal page, then click the **OK** button to save the change and close the **Internet Options** dialog box.

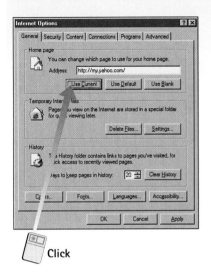

Click

5 Load Your New Home Page

Click the **Home** button at any time to return to your customized portal page.

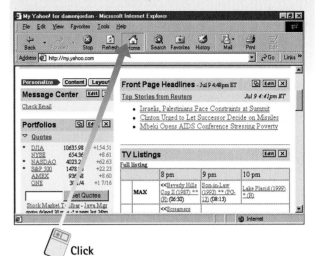

Click

6 Restore the Original

If you change your mind and want to return to Internet Explorer's original home page, open the **Internet Options** dialog box, click the **Use Default** button, then click the **OK** button.

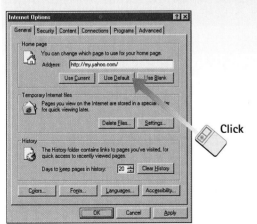

Click

End

Task

4

Searching the World Wide Web

*T*he World Wide Web has an unbelievable amount of useful information, whether you're using it as a student, consumer, worker, researcher, or entertainment seeker.

The Web offers important health advisories such as food recall warnings at the U.S. Food and Drug Administration site, investment advice at numerous stock-analysis and news sites, constantly updated news, homework helpers, and thousands of pages devoted to hobbies. But none of this information is any help to you if you can't find it.

You can search the World Wide Web in two ways—exploring Web directories and relying on search engines.

Directories such as Yahoo! and the Open Directory Project attempt to impose some order on the chaos of the Web, recruiting editors to prepare lists of related sites in a very structured manner. Sites are categorized in a well-organized hierarchy, making it easier to find a bunch of different sites related to the same subject matter.

Search engines are massive databases that attempt to index the entire Web. These databases are prepared by machines instead of humans. You can use these search engines to search for text on millions of Web pages at once, relying on the search engine to find the most appropriate pages.

If you want to conduct an effective search for information, you should use both methods. ●

How to Find a Site When You Don't Know Its Address

Every document on the World Wide Web has a unique address called a URL, which is short for *uniform resource locator.* A site's address can take many forms, but most of the largest Web sites have similar-looking and simple URLs, such as `http://www.yahoo.com`, `http://www.microsoft.com`, `http://www.cmp.net`, `http://www.slashdot.org`, `http://www.nasa.gov`, and `http://www.mit.edu`. By learning a few things about these addresses, you can make an educated guess about the addresses of some of the Web sites you're looking for.

Begin

1 Look for a Company's Address

The most popular ending used in a Web address is `.com`. If you know the name of a company or publication, you can try to find its Web site by typing the following into Internet Explorer 5's Address bar: `http://www.` followed by the company name, followed by `.com`. Press **Enter** to see whether the browser can find a site at that address. One example: Dell Computer Corp. is at `http://www.dell.com`.

2 Try a Shorter Address

Some sites with addresses ending in `.com` don't start with the `http://www.` prefix. You can also look for a company or publication's address by typing the name followed by `.com` in the Address bar and then pressing **Enter**. One example: `http://monster.com`.

3 Look for an Organization

Many Web addresses that end in `.org` are not-for-profit organizations (although this is not a requirement). Look for an organization by typing `http://www.` in the Address bar, followed by the group's name, followed by `.org`. Press **Enter** after typing the full address.

4 Look for a Government Site

All Web addresses that end in **.gov** are affiliated with the United States government. One of the most popular is **http://www.whitehouse.gov**, the White House site. To look for a government agency or similar entity, type **http://www.** in the Address bar, then type the group's name, then type **.gov** and press **Enter**.

5 Autosearch for the Name

Internet Explorer 5 has an Autosearch feature that searches for keywords you type in the Address bar. Type the name of the entity you're looking for in the Address bar. As you are typing, a text box appears below the Address bar, describing what you are looking for. Press **Enter** to begin the search.

6 View the Search Results

Autosearch opens two windows in your browser: a list of sites recommended by the Microsoft Network that may match the name, and a window containing the best-matching site—if one can be found. Click a hyperlink to a site in the **Auto-Search** window (the left pane) to load the associated page.

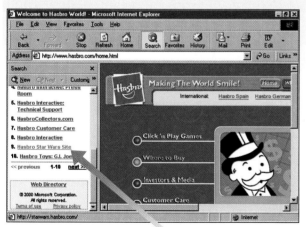

 Click

End

How-To Hints

Finding Universities and Colleges

Learning another type of Web address can help you locate the sites of colleges, universities, and advanced research institutions. These institutions almost always have Web sites that end with **.edu**; in the Address bar, type **http://www.**, then the name of the institution, then **.edu**, and press **Enter**. For example, **http://www.psu.edu** is the home page of Penn State University.

Shortening the Addresses of Web Pages

The URL associated with a Web page is usually prefaced with **http://** (which indicates the protocol used to send the page to your browser). Another common prefix is **ftp://**. The current crop of browsers (including Internet Explorer 5) will add **http://** automatically if you forget to include **http://** or **ftp://** in a URL. For this reason, you can type a URL such as **www.dell.com** instead of **http://www.dell.com**.

How to See Pages You Have Recently Visited

If you haven't turned off the feature, Internet Explorer 5 can keep track of the sites you've visited in recent days. This list is stored in the History list, which is presented in a manner similar to the browser's Favorites list. By default, Internet Explorer keeps track of all sites visited in the past 20 days. If you're searching for something you have recently viewed, the place to start looking for it is your browser's History list.

Begin

1 Open the History List

Click the **History** button to open a window containing the History list.

Click

2 Open a Site's Hyperlinks

Each folder in the History list is devoted to a Web site you visited on a specific day. Open a folder by clicking it. You'll see Internet shortcuts for every page on that site you visited during the day.

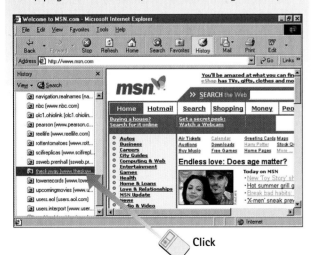

Click

3 Revisit a Web Site

To revisit a Web page, double-click its Internet shortcut in the History list. The page is loaded in a browser window.

 Double-click

4 Search for a Shortcut

Looking through the History list by hand can be time consuming if you have visited a large number of Web sites. To search through the entire list, click the **Search** button in the bar above the History list.

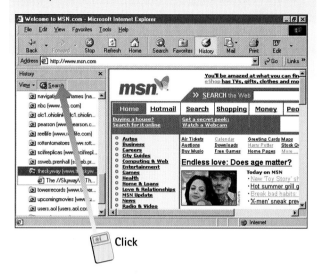

Click

5 Conduct the Search

Enter the text you're looking for in the **Search for** box and click the **Search Now** button. All items in the History list that match the search text will be displayed.

Click

6 Delete History Items

To remove a folder or shortcut from the History list, right-click the item and choose **Delete** from the context menu. (You also can delete all shortcuts in the entire History list: Pull down the **Tools** menu, choose **Internet Options**, and click the **Clear History** button to delete them.)

Right-click

7 Rearrange History Items

Normally, items in the History list are organized by date. To arrange the list according to how often you visit pages, click the **View** button in the bar above the History list and choose the **By Most Visited** command.

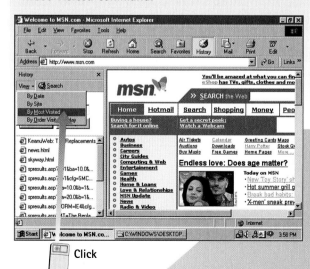

Click

End

How to Search for a Specific Topic on the Web

There are several ways to search for sites related to a specific topic on the World Wide Web. Task 2, "How to Visit a Web Site When You Know Its Address," in Part 2, "Browsing the World Wide Web," describes how to use Internet Explorer 5's **Autosearch** feature to search for sites by entering a topic in the browser's Address bar. Another way to search by topic is to use the World Wide Web directories published by Yahoo!, Excite, the Open Directory Project, and others.

Begin

1 Visit a Directory

Most Web directories function in a similar manner. The Open Directory Project is a volunteer effort coordinated by Netscape that organizes more than 600,000 sites into categories. To visit the site, type **http://www.dmoz.org** into Internet Explorer's Address bar and press **Enter**.

2 Search for a Topic

Type the topic you're looking for in the site's search box and click the **Search** button.

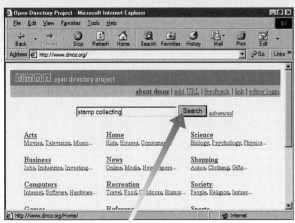

 Click

3 View the Results

Web directories are organized into categories—pages that contain Web sites and links to subcategories. Categories that match your topic are listed first in the search results page and are usually the best place to find what you're looking for. To view a category, click its hyperlink in the results page.

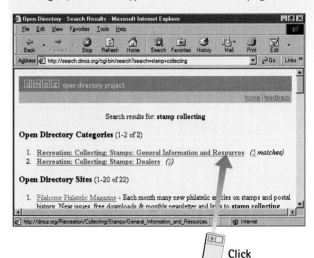

Click

4 Scan a Category

Category pages display all subcategories and Web sites that match a given topic. Click a hyperlink to visit the associated site.

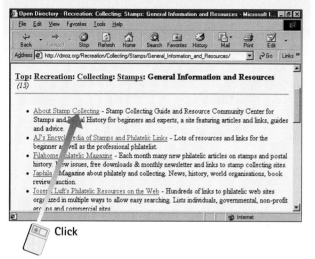

Click

5 Scan Page Links

When you search a Web directory, Web pages about your topic are listed after any matching categories. Click a hyperlink to visit one of these sites.

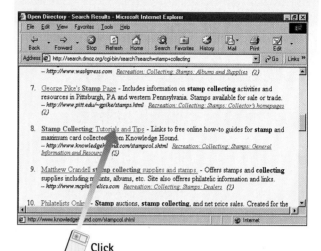

Click

6 Search Within a Category

When you're viewing a category page, you can conduct a new search that is confined to the portion of the directory that's related to the category. Type a search topic in the search box, pull down the drop-down menu, and select the **Only In <category>** option; then click the **Search** button.

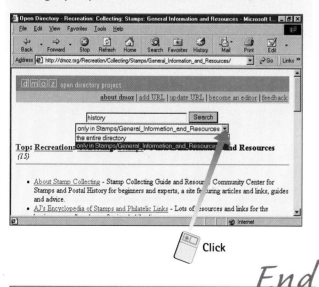

Click

End

How-To Hints

Using Other Web Directories

Each Web directory includes a different selection of Web sites, so you may want to try several directories. Use the following URLs to visit some of the other popular services:

- ✓ **Yahoo!**: http://www.yahoo.com
- ✓ **Lycos**: http://www.lycos.com
- ✓ **Excite**: http://www.excite.com
- ✓ **Snap!**: http://www.snap.com

Broadening Your Search

In the Open Directory Project and other directories, every category name includes hyperlinks to broader categories with which it is associated—for example, the `Top:Recreation:Collecting:Stamps` category is a subcategory of the more general `Top:Recreation:Collecting` category. Use these links to make your search *less* specific.

How to Search Through Millions of Web Pages

The World Wide Web grows at a speed much faster than any human-compiled directory can possibly match. For this reason, you can search through millions of machine-compiled pages by visiting a *search engine*. Search engines are massive databases containing the text of documents available on the Web. These engines continuously traverse links on the World Wide Web, adding new documents and deleting those that have been taken offline. Some of the most popular search engines are AltaVista, HotBot, Northern Light, and Google.

Begin

1 Visit a Search Engine

One of the largest search engines is AltaVista, which was founded by DEC in 1995 and is now a subsidiary of Compaq. To visit this engine, type **http://www.altavista.com** into the Address bar and press **Enter**.

3 View the Search Results

Search engines rank the best-matching pages first. The engine ignores all common words you use (such as *the* or *and*) and ranks pages according to the number of other search words that were found. You can use the **Next** hyperlink at the bottom of a page to view more results. Click a page's title to visit that page.

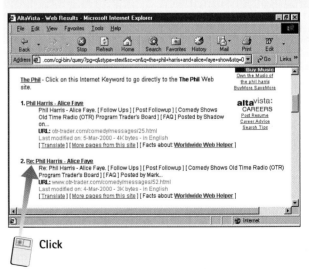

Click

2 Conduct a Search

To search AltaVista, type a question, sentence, or phrase describing what you're looking for into the search box. Be as specific as possible. Click the **Search** button to begin looking.

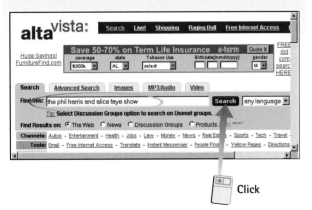

Click

4 Conduct an Advanced Search

AltaVista puts its advanced search features on a separate page. Click the **Advanced Search** tab hyperlink on the site's home page to conduct more complex searches.

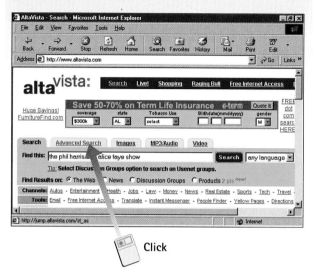

Click

5 Search for a Specific Phrase

The **Enter boolean expression** box is used to conduct targeted searches. To look for a specific phrase, type it in the box with quotation marks around the phrase, and then click the **Search** button. The search results include only those pages that contain this exact phrase.

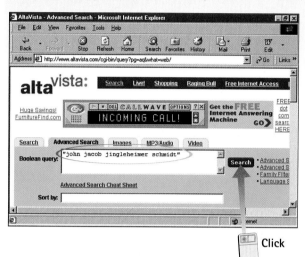

Click

6 Search for Text in a Page Title

A Web page's title often contains a succinct description of its contents. To search through page titles, in the **Enter boolean expression** box type the text **title:**, followed by the text you're looking for. If you're looking for a phrase, place quotation marks around the phrase. Click the **Search** button to view results.

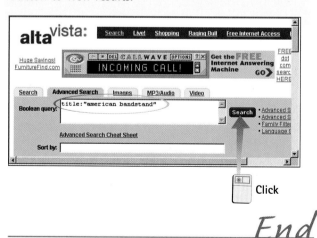

Click

End

How-To Hints

Visiting Other Search Engines

By recent estimates, even search engines can't keep up with how fast the World Wide Web is growing. To use some of the other search engines, visit the following Web sites:

✓ **HotBot**: http://www.hotbot.com

✓ **Google**: http://www.google.com

✓ **Northern Light**:
http://www.northernlight.com

✓ **MetaCrawler**:
http://www.metacrawler.com

✓ **WebCrawler**:
http://www.webcrawler.com

✓ **Lycos**: www.lycos.com

How to Find a Program on the Web

As you might expect, World Wide Web users are a natural audience to do their computer software shopping online. You can use the Web to purchase software, receive and install demo versions of software, and choose from thousands of useful free computer programs. One site that offers each of these services is Download.com, published by CNET. The name comes from the term *download*, which means to transmit a file from another network to your system.

Begin

1 Visit the Site

To get started, type **http://www.download.com** in Internet Explorer 5's Address bar and press **Enter**. The Download.com home page opens in your browser window.

2 Search for Software

Programs you can try before you buy are called *shareware*, and Download.com offers thousands of shareware items you can download. To search for a program, type its name in the **Search** box, choose **In Downloads** from the **In** drop-down list, and click the **Search** button.

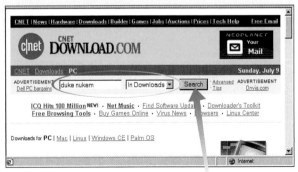

 Click

3 Explore Search Results

Download.com lists all programs that match the name you're looking for. To find out more about a specific program, click its hyperlink.

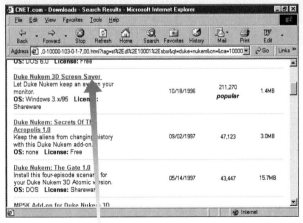

 Click

4 Download a Program

If you decide that you want to download the program whose description you have been reading, click the **Download Now** hyperlink. The **File Download** dialog box opens.

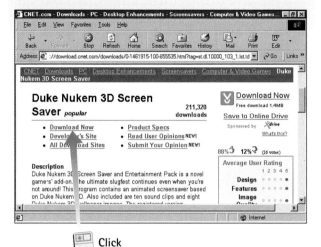

Click

5 Choose a Download Method

When you're downloading a program, you can save it in a folder on your system or run it immediately. If you save a program to a folder, after the download is finished, click the program's icon to begin installation. To run the program without saving it on your own system, click the **Run this program from its current location** option.

Click

6 Look for Retail Software

To find commercial software that you can't download—such as the software sold at computer superstores—click the **Prices** hyperlink on the Download.com menu at the top of the home page.

Click

7 Begin a Search

Type the software's name in the **Search** box, choose **In Shopping**, and click the **Go!** button. Download.com will compare prices on that commercial software product at several different online software stores, displaying the results in tabular form on a new Web page.

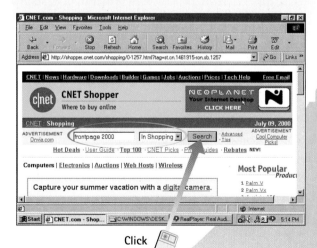

Click

End

How to Find a Company on the Web

Today, most companies that do business on a national or international scale have a World Wide Web site. Thousands of smaller local companies also are online, making the Web a great place to look up companies, buy their products, and seek customer support. You can find a company using the techniques introduced in Tasks 1 and 2, earlier in this part. There also are a few ways to speed up your search.

Begin

1 Use Autosearch

Internet Explorer 5's **Autosearch** feature can direct you to many company sites. Type the company's name in the Address bar and press **Enter**.

2 View the Results

Autosearch opens two windows: one containing a list of possible sites that match the text you type, and another containing the best match (if Autosearch can find one). Click a hyperlink in the **Autosearch** window to load that site.

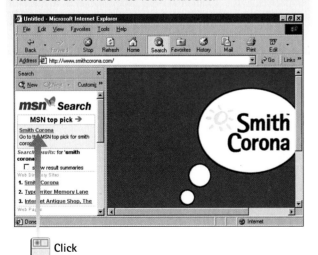

Click

3 Search Yahoo!

Another good source for company sites is Yahoo!. Type **www.yahoo.com** in the browser's Address bar and press **Enter**. When the home page opens, type the name of the company you are looking for in the search box and click the **Search** button.

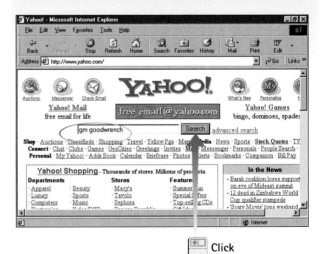

Click

4 View Yahoo! Results

Yahoo! lists all categories and Web sites that match the name you typed, with the best matches displayed first. Click a hyperlink to visit the associated Web site.

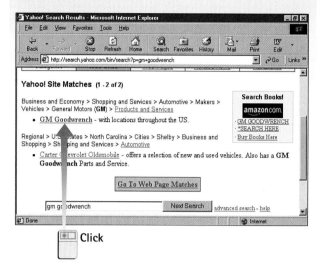

Click

5 Use RealNames

The AltaVista search engine is useful for company searches because it incorporates Real-Names, a database that serves a similar purpose to the Autosearch feature. Type **http://www.altavista.com** in the Address bar and press **Enter** to go to the AltaVista home page. Once you're there, type the company name in the search box and click the **Search** button.

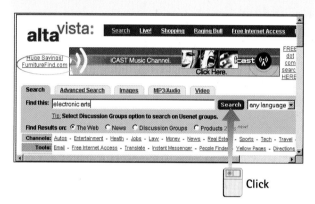

Click

6 Use the RealNames Link

The first item listed on an AltaVista search results page is a hyperlink to the RealNames database. If RealNames reports an exact match, click the link to visit that company's site. If the match is not exact, click a link to see the best-available matches that RealNames can find.

Click

7 View Related Links

When an exact match is not found, RealNames lists several of the best-available match-es. Click the hyperlink of one of these alternative finds to see whether it's what you're looking for. In this example, there was no matching RealName for the term *bullwinkle*, so several different sites involving the search term were recommended.

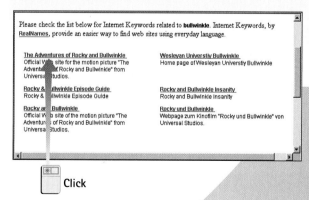

Click

End

How to Find a Person on the Web

You can search for people just as you do any other subject on the World Wide Web: using Web directories such as Yahoo! and search engines such as AltaVista and Google. A more focused search is available using directories such as Yahoo! People Search (a mailing address and email directory). People Search scans a collection of public databases for matching names and can be narrowed to specific states or provinces. People Search also links to other public directories, such as 1800USSearch.com.

Begin

1 Search for a Phone Number

Open the Yahoo! People Search home page by entering **http://people.yahoo.com** in your browser's Address bar and pressing **Enter**. To search the entire database for someone's phone number, type the person's first and last names in the **Telephone Search** boxes and then click the **Search** button. You can omit the first name to see all matches for a surname.

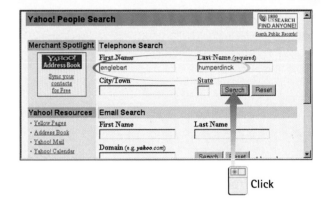

Click

2 Narrow Your Search

If you want to narrow your search to a single state, type the state's postal abbreviation in the **State** box. Click **Search** to look for a match.

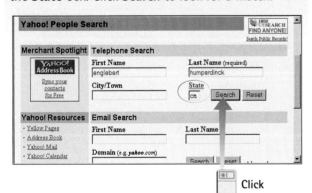

Click

3 Search for an Email Address

To look for someone's email address, type the person's first and last names in the **Email Search** boxes and then click the adjacent **Search** button.

Click

4 Modify Your Email Search

You can omit the person's first name to conduct a search based only on the surname. There also are ways to narrow a search: If you know the domain someone is using, type it in the **Domain** box. Click **Search** to see a page displaying the email addresses and names of people who match the search text.

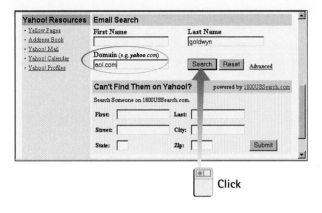

Click

5 Make an Advanced Email Search

Yahoo! People Search offers even more options for email searches. Click the **Advanced** hyperlink to load the more sophisticated search page.

Click

6 Fill Out the Search Form

Most fields in the **Advanced Search** page can be used to narrow a search. You can pick the state or province, country, former email address, and organization type. Check the **SmartNames** box to treat related first names (such as Bill, Billy, and William) as the same name. Click the **Search** button when you're ready to search.

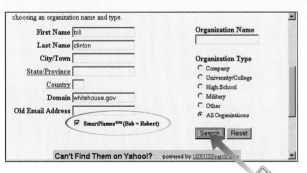

Click

End

How-To Hints

Finding Email Addresses on Usenet

Usenet (a collection of discussion forums on more than 20,000 topics) attracts thousands of Internet users who post messages that contain their email addresses. You can search Deja.com, an archive of Usenet messages, for a specific person. To visit the database, type **www.deja.com** into your browser's Address bar and press **Enter**. You learn more about searching this archive in Part 7, Task 6, "How to Search an Archive of Past Newsgroup Discussions."

Task

Protecting Yourself on the Web

*P*art of the World Wide Web's appeal is its wide-open nature. There has never been a mass medium before with so few barriers between a publisher and an audience. Anyone can put a site on the Web and reach people all over the world at little or no cost.

This has its advantages—free speech is exercised on the Internet with great success. This also has its disadvantages—content that some people find objectionable is available on the World Wide Web in great quantity.

Web pages can contain interactive programs written with languages such as Java and technology such as ActiveX. These programs can sometimes expose security holes that put your own computer at risk.

Files you receive over the Web also can contain *viruses*—small programs that secretly copy themselves to different disks on your computer. Because viruses may intentionally damage files and programs, Internet Explorer can be set up to warn you before any file is run from the browser.

When you run a program in a Web browser, it's running on *your* computer just like any other software you use. For this reason, browsers such as Internet Explorer 5 have security settings that restrict the ways a page can interact with your system. By adjusting these settings, you can reduce the risks of using the Web. ●

How to Choose a Security Setting

Although security risks are extremely small on the World Wide Web, you may encounter sites that try to damage files on your computer or steal confidential data. Internet Explorer 5's security settings can restrict or disable browser features that are most susceptible to abuse, such as JavaScript, Active Scripting, Java, and cookies. Restricting these features can limit your enjoyment of the Web because many popular sites rely on them, but you may feel it's a fair trade-off for a more secure computer system.

Begin

1 Configure Your Browser

To get started, pull down the Internet Explorer **Tools** menu and select the **Internet Options** command. The **Internet Options** dialog box opens.

Click

2 View Security Settings

Click the **Security** tab to view your current security settings and to make changes to those settings.

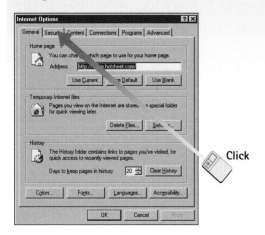

Click

3 Set Your Internet Security

Internet Explorer enables different levels of security for sites on the Internet and sites on a local *intranet*—a private network of documents shared by people in a company, school, or organization. To change your Internet settings, click the **Internet** icon from the **Select a Web content zone to specify its security settings** list box.

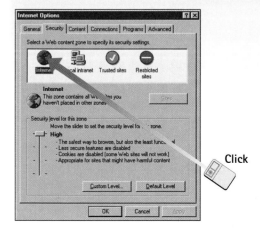

Click

4 Pick a Security Level

There are four basic security levels: **High**, **Medium**, **Medium-Low**, and **Low**. These levels determine the kind of content Internet Explorer will load and the tasks it will restrict. To choose a security level, drag the slider to that level and release it. The How-To Hints box at the end of this task provides some guidelines for setting a security level.

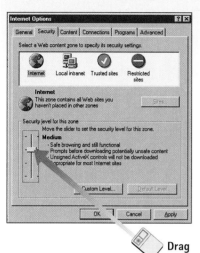

Drag

5 Oppose a Recommendation

Microsoft recommends that you use **High** or **Medium** security while browsing the Internet. If you choose lower security, a dialog box appears, asking you to confirm this choice. Click **Yes** if you want to disregard Microsoft's recommendation and choose a lower security level.

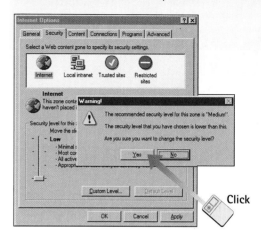

Click

6 Restore the Default Level

If you want to restore your browser security to the level recommended by Microsoft, click the **Default Level** button.

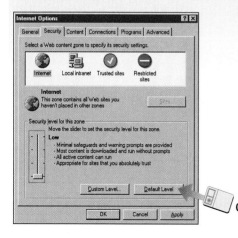

Click

How-To Hints

Deciding on a Security Level

If you're not a Web site developer, you probably won't have much to go on when choosing a security level. To help guide your decision, try **High** security first. As you're visiting Web sites afterward, your browser and some sites will often tell you what you're missing out on because of your security level. You can then repeat the steps in this task and select a slightly lower security level if you want to access some of the features you've been missing.

End

How to Customize Your Security Setting

For most people, Internet Explorer 5's basic security levels should be sufficient. If you want more control over your browser's security, you can customize each of its security settings. This enables you to turn on and off specific features such as cookies, Java, JavaScript, and file download—and turn off some browser security warnings as well. Doing this can cause security risks, so you should be cautious about making drastic changes.

Begin

1 Change Your Settings

Pull down the **Tools** menu and select the **Internet Options** command to open the **Internet Options** dialog box and view your Internet Explorer settings.

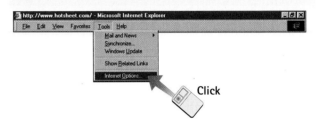

Click

2 Choose a Custom Level

If the **Security** tab is not on top, click that tab to see your current security settings. To change how your browser handles specific security issues, click the **Custom Level** button. The **Security Settings** dialog box opens.

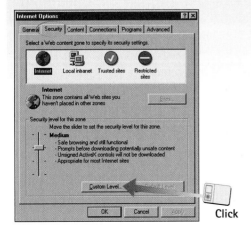

Click

3 Set Up a Custom Level

By default, custom settings are identical to those specified by the **Medium** security level. To make them identical to a different level, click the down arrow next to the **Reset to** box and select the level you want to use as a starting point.

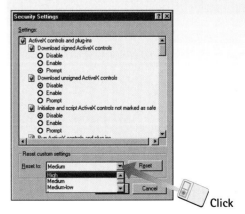

Click

4 Reset All Settings

Click the **Reset** button to make all custom settings the same as the level shown in the **Reset to** box.

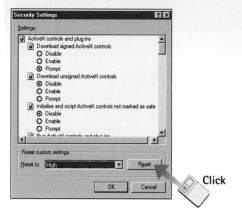

Click

5 Customize Your Settings

Scroll through the **Settings** box to see the various settings you can affect. To change a specific setting, click the appropriate radio button. Click **Disable** to turn off a feature, **Enable** to turn on a feature, and **Prompt** if the browser should ask whether a feature should be used each time it is encountered on a Web page. Click **OK** to save all your changes.

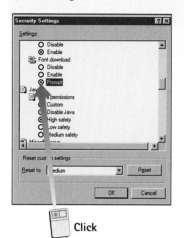

Click

6 Undo Customization

To remove a custom security level and undo all the changes you have made since opening the **Internet Options** dialog box, return to the **Security** tab of the **Internet Options** dialog box and click the **Default Level** button.

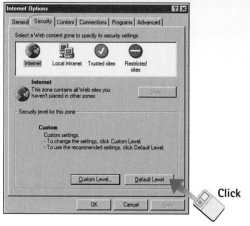

Click

How-To Hints

Turning Off Form Warnings

By default, Internet Explorer warns you before it sends data you've entered on a form that's located on an unencrypted Web server. This feature keeps you from sending private information (such as your credit card number) without *encryption*—a way to encode data so that it remains confidential. This warning is cumbersome if you're one of those people who never reveals personal data on the Web. To turn off this warning, find the **Submit Nonencrypted Form Data** setting in your custom settings (see Step 5) and click the **Disable** radio button.

End

How to Block Objectionable Content from Being Viewed

To place restrictions on the material that can be viewed with Internet Explorer 5, use the browser's Content Advisor. The Advisor relies on RSACi ratings—an industry standard adopted voluntarily by some Web publishers to indicate their site's level of objectionable language, nudity, sex, and violence. Although the Content Advisor is far from foolproof—it relies on Web sites that honestly assess their own content—you may find it useful in conjunction with other methods of filtering the Web.

2 Choose a Password

The first thing you must do is select a supervisor password. This password can be used at any time to change Content Advisor settings or turn it off completely. After you set up a password, you can't modify how the Content Advisor works without it. Enter your password in both text boxes and click **OK** to close this window and return to the **Internet Options** dialog box.

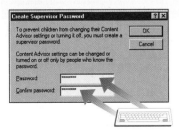

Begin

1 View Content Settings

The Content Advisor is configured with all other browser settings. Choose **Tools, Internet Options** from the menu bar to open the **Internet Options** dialog box. Click the **Content** tab to view the browser's content settings. To set up the Content Advisor, first click the **Enable** button. The **Create Supervisor Password** dialog box opens.

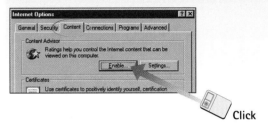

Click

3 Set Your Content Ratings

On the **Content** tab of the **Internet Options** dialog box, click the **Enable** button. The **Content Advisor** dialog box opens to the **Ratings** tab, ready for you to set your browser's acceptable RSACi rating. Click the RSACi category you want to set, then drag the slider to a content setting. A site must have content rated at or below all four settings to pass the Content Advisor. Pages that don't pass are not displayed.

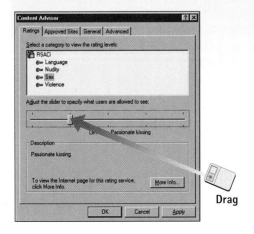

Drag

4 View Unrated Sites

By default, Web pages without RSACi ratings cannot be viewed. This keeps out unrated sites that contain objectionable material, along with thousands of sites that don't participate in RSACi. To allow unrated sites to be viewed, click the **General** tab of the **Content Advisor** dialog box and select the **Users can see sites that have no rating** option.

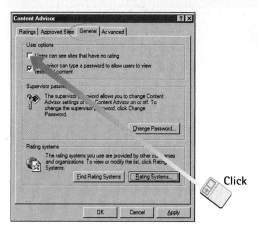

Click

5 Approve Individual Sites

To allow individual sites to bypass the Content Advisor, click the **Approved Sites** tab, type the site's main address in the **Allow this Web site** text box, and click the **Always** button. You can completely restrict access to the site by clicking the **Never** button instead.

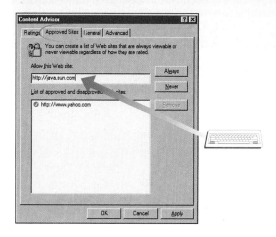

6 Save Your Changes

Click the **OK** button to save your new settings and close the **Content Advisor** dialog box. Click **OK** again to close the **Internet Options** dialog box. If you have imposed content restrictions, you should close Internet Explorer and launch it again. This action keeps recently visited sites from being reloaded without first being checked by the Content Advisor.

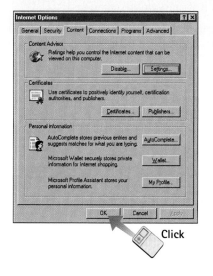

Click

7 Turn Off the Content Advisor

To turn off the Content Advisor completely, choose **Tools**, **Internet Options** to open the **Internet Options** dialog box. On the **Content** tab, click the **Disable** button. The supervisor password is required before the feature is actually turned off.

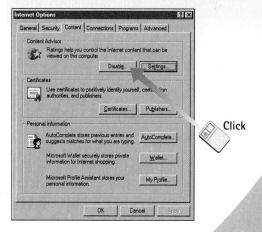

Click

End

How to Use Security Certificates

As you are visiting World Wide Web sites, you may come across pages that contain interactive programs. These programs are downloaded to your computer and then run as if you installed them from a CD-ROM, although they are much smaller than commercial software. Programs written using ActiveX technology must be approved before your Web browser runs them. Internet Explorer 5 presents a *security certificate*—a special browser window vouching for the authenticity of the program's author. You must examine this certificate and decide whether to let the program run.

Begin

1 Inspect a Certificate

When you load a page that contains a new ActiveX control, Internet Explorer presents a dialog box asking whether the control should be installed. The author of the program is presented as a hyperlink. Click this hyperlink to find out more about the author.

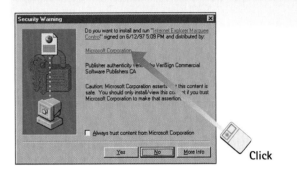

Click

2 Determine Authenticity

The hyperlink opens a security certificate associated with the author of the ActiveX control. Companies such as VeriSign and Thawte create these certificates after verifying the authorship of the program. Click each of the tabs on this window to find out more about the certificate and the control's author. Click the **OK** button to close the certificate window.

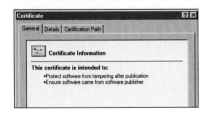

3 Always Trust an Author

If you are comfortable with the control's authorship, you can automatically approve any controls that author creates in the future. Select the **Always trust content label** option if you want. (**Note:** It's safer to approve controls individually than to issue blanket approval with this check box.)

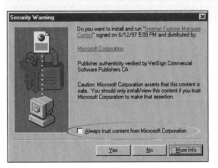

4 Reject an Author

To prevent an ActiveX control from being installed, click the **No** button in the **Security Warning** dialog box. You can still use anything on the current Web page that doesn't rely on the ActiveX control.

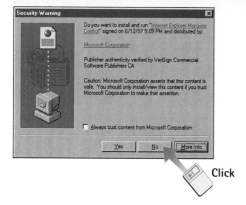

Click

5 Approve an Author

To approve an ActiveX control and cause it to be run by your browser, click the **Yes** button. The control will be saved on your system in the Windows/Downloaded Program Files folder so that it doesn't have to be installed again every time you visit the page.

Click

End

How-To Hints

Restricting ActiveX Controls on Your Browser

If you are never asked whether an ActiveX control should be installed before it starts running on a Web page, your browser may be configured with a low security level. To check your security settings, select **Tools, Internet Options** to open the **Internet Options** dialog box and click the **Security** tab. Refer to Tasks 1 and 2 in this part of the book for instructions on setting and customizing a security level in Internet Explorer.

How to Disable Cookies in a Web Browser

Web sites can keep track of who's visiting them by using *cookies*—small files that contain information collected by a site. Internet Explorer 5 will save any site's cookie file on your computer and send that same file back to the site whenever you visit it again. The cookie file can be used to store personal information such as your name, billing information for a site you buy products from, and similar data. By design, Internet Explorer sends a cookie file that exists on your computer only to the site that created it. Some Web sites require cookie files, but you can turn them off entirely by adjusting the browser's security settings.

Begin

1 Change Your Settings

The first step is to select **Tools, Internet Options**. The **Internet Options** dialog box opens to the **General** tab, displaying how your browser is configured.

Click

2 View Security Settings

Click the **Security** tab to bring its settings to the front of the dialog box.

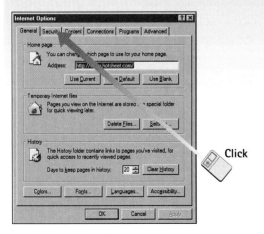

Click

3 Customize Your Security

Turning off cookies requires that you customize your browser's security level. Click the **Custom Level** button to open the **Security Settings** dialog box so that you can begin customizing security options.

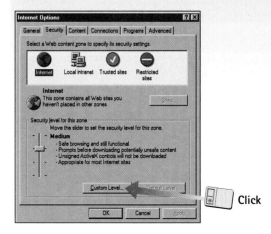

Click

4 Disable Permanent Cookies

Scroll through the options in the **Settings** list box until you locate the **Cookies** options. To prevent cookie files from being permanently saved on your computer, click the **Disable** radio button under **Allow cookies that are stored on your computer**.

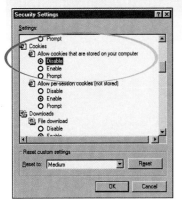

5 Disable Session Cookies

To disable temporary cookies, click the **Disable** button under the **Allow per-session cookies** option. The cookies that are used during your online session will then be automatically deleted when you close Internet Explorer. Disabling session cookies prevents the files from being created on your system.

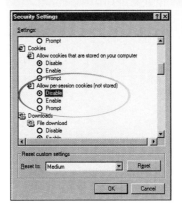

End

How-To Hints

Approving Cookies on a Case-by-Case Basis

The security settings for cookies each have a **Prompt** option. If you choose **Prompt** instead of **Disable**, Internet Explorer will ask for permission to save a cookie every time a Web site presents one. The **Prompt** option provides a way to use some cookie-reliant Web sites while blocking others. Note, however, that this option is more time consuming than the **Disable** and **Enable** options—you'll be asked for permission often while visiting Web sites.

Task

Part 6

Communicating with Electronic Mail

*I*n the technology industry, one term marketers use to describe a product is a *killer app*, which is short for *killer application*. A killer app is a must-have feature—the main reason a consumer buys a specific product. For many people, the killer app of the Internet is one of the services that has been around the longest: electronic mail.

Electronic mail, more commonly called *email*, enables you to send messages to anyone who has an Internet email address. These messages, which are almost always free to send and to receive, usually arrive within seconds or minutes of being sent.

Using email, you can communicate directly with friends, family members, and colleagues. You can send messages to your elected leaders, request customer support from a business, and exchange pictures and other files. You also can receive advertisements, although unfortunately many of these arrive unsolicited—a type of Internet marketing called *spam*.

Most Internet service providers offer an email account as part of your subscription. (One of the things you must obtain from your provider is the information necessary to use your new email account: your username and password, the name of your provider's mail servers, and other setup details.) In addition, a growing number of Web sites are offering free lifetime email accounts, such as Microsoft Hotmail and Prontomail.

Sending and receiving email requires an account and software that can send and receive messages. The following tasks cover all the basics of using an email account. ●

How to Set Up Outlook Express for Email

Windows and Internet Explorer 5 come with Microsoft Outlook Express, a popular email program that can send and deliver email and manage an email address book. Before you can set up Outlook Express, you must have the following information from your Internet service provider: your username and password, the incoming mail server's name, the outgoing mail server's name, and the type of incoming mail server you'll be accessing (POP3, IMAP, or HTTP). Most incoming servers use a protocol called POP3.

Begin

1 Run Outlook Express

To begin, click the **Start** menu and choose **Programs**, **Outlook Express**. There also may be an **Outlook Express** icon on your desktop; if there is, double-click this icon. The Outlook Express program opens.

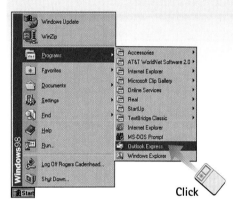

Click

2 Create a New Account

Outlook Express may have already been set up to send and receive email—some online services handle this during the signup process. If Outlook Express has not been set up already, a **Set up a Mail account** hyperlink is displayed in the program's main window. Click this hyperlink to open the **Internet Connection Wizard** and begin setting up an account.

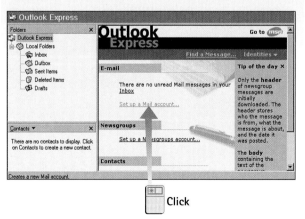

Click

3 Identify Yourself

In the **Display name** text box, type a name (also called a *handle*) that will identify you on all outgoing mail; click **Next**. This name is displayed in addition to your email address on all email that you send. Most people use their full name as their handle.

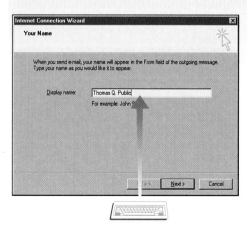

4 Set Up an Email Address

If you have a new email address provided by your Internet service (or an existing email address) you'd like to continue using, type it into the **E-mail address** text box and click the **Next** button. (The **I'd like to sign up for a new account** option is described in Task 8, "How to Set Up a Free Web-Based Email Account.")

5 Identify Your Servers

If your Internet service provider supports email, you should have been given the names of its mail servers when you joined the service. Type the names of its mail servers in the **Incoming mail** and **Outgoing mail** text boxes. Use the drop-down list to indicate the kind of incoming server being used (most services use POP3). Click **Next** to continue.

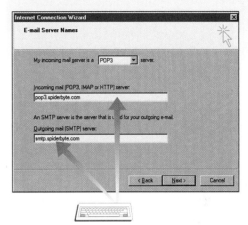

6 Enter Your Account Info

You must have a username and password to make use of Internet email servers. (You get this information from your Internet service provider.) Type these into the **Account name** and **Password** text boxes, checking the **Remember password** box if you want Outlook Express to log into your account automatically.

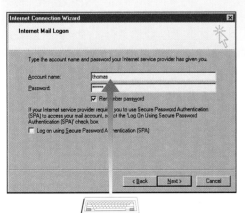

7 Set Up Authentication

If your Internet service requires it, check the **Log on using Secure Password Authentication (SPA)** option. To finish setting up Outlook Express to work with your email address, click the **Next** button and then click the **Finish** button.

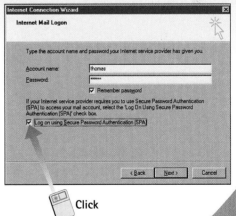

Click

End

TASK 2

How to Send Email

Writing a message in Outlook Express is similar to creating a document in a word processor such as Microsoft Word. You type the text of your message and apply formatting with familiar toolbar buttons such as Bold and Italics. Outlook Express normally composes email with HTML so that your messages can contain fonts, graphics, and formatting just like World Wide Web pages. Because your recipient must be able to read HTML mail to see all these features, you can turn off HTML and send a message as a simple text file.

Begin

1 Create a New Message

Click the **Start** menu and choose **Programs**, **Outlook Express** to launch Outlook Express. To begin writing a new message, click the **new Mail message** hyperlink. The New Message window opens.

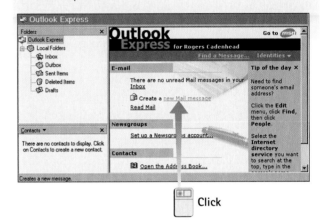

Click

2 Address the Message

Type the email address of the message's recipient in the **To** text box. If you're sending a copy of this message to another email address, type that address in the **Cc** text box. Finish addressing the message by typing a short title for the message in the **Subject** box.

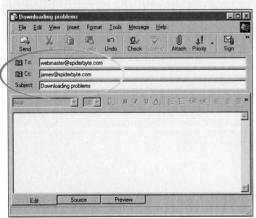

3 Write the Message

Type the text of your message in the edit pane. If you're sending a message that should not contain any HTML formatting, pull down the **Format** menu (located above the edit pane) and choose the **Plain Text** option.

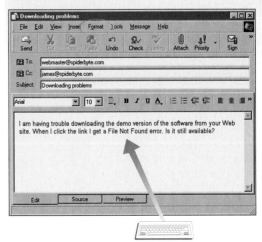

80   PART 6: COMMUNICATING WITH ELECTRONIC MAIL

4 Format the Message

Messages you send with HTML formatting can contain different fonts, bold text, a graphical background, and other visual touches. These features are available on the toolbar above the edit pane. To make text bold, for example, select the text by dragging your mouse over it and then click the **Bold** button in the toolbar.

Click

5 Set a Priority

To assign a priority to your message, click the arrow next to the **Priority** button in the toolbar at the top of the window and choose **High Priority**, **Normal Priority**, or **Low Priority**. The priority setting does not cause the message to be delivered any differently, but the priority rating may be noted by the recipient's email program when the message is displayed.

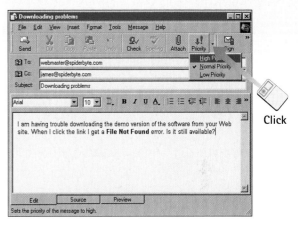

Click

6 Send the Message

When your message has been addressed, typed, and formatted the way you want it, click the **Send** button to deliver the email message. A copy of the message is stored in the **Sent Items** folder of Outlook Express.

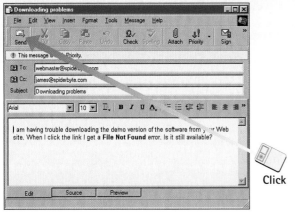

Click

End

How-To Hints

Making Use of HTML Formatting

Most email programs handle only plain text—letters, numbers, and punctuation without any special formatting. Outlook Express, Hotmail, and other email services are starting to support email that contains HTML—the same kind of formatting used to create Web pages. To add images, colors, or sound to the background of your email message in Outlook Express, choose **Format**, **Background**, and select the **Picture**, **Color**, or **Sound** command. This special formatting may make your message unreadable if your recipient can't handle HTML-formatted email. For this reason, use special formatting only if you know that the recipient's email program supports it.

How to Receive Email

Every time you run Outlook Express, the program connects to your Internet service's incoming mail server and checks for new messages for you. Outlook Express is organized like a file folder, and it contains subfolders for **Inbox**, **Outbox**, **Sent Items**, **Deleted Items**, and **Drafts**. New messages are placed in your **Inbox**, where they stay until you move them to a new folder or delete them. If you are also using Hotmail, an extra set of folders exists for mail received with that service. (You learn more about Hotmail in Task 8, "How to Set Up a Free Web-Based Email Account.")

Begin

1 Read Unread Mail

Click the **Start** menu and choose **Programs**, **Outlook Express** to launch Outlook Express. If any new email has been received, click the **unread Mail message** hyperlink to see the messages you have. Alternatively, you can click the **Inbox** item in the **Local Folders** list to see messages you have read previously.

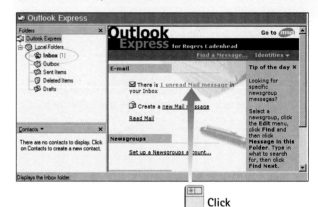

Click

2 View Messages

The top-right pane of the **Inbox** window lists all messages in the folder—new, unread messages and messages you've read previously. You can use the scrollbar to move through this list. Click a message's icon to view its contents in the bottom-right pane. To delete a message, click its icon in the top-right pane and then click the **Delete** button.

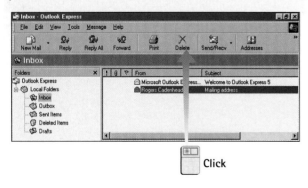

Click

3 View a Message in a New Window

The bottom-right pane of the **Inbox** window doesn't have a lot of room to display a message. To view a message in a larger window, double-click the message in the top-right pane of the **Inbox** window. A new window appears, with the selected message displayed.

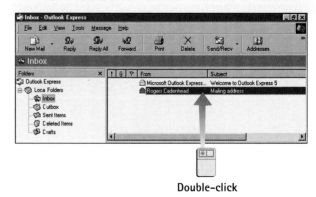

Double-click

4 View Other Messages

As you're viewing a message in its own window, you can use the **Previous** and **Next** buttons in the toolbar at the top of the window to see other messages in the same folder. Click the **Next** button to view the next message in your Outlook Express **Inbox**.

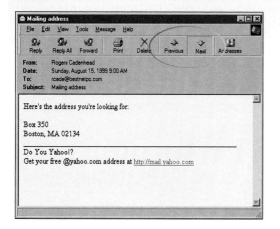

5 Reply to a Message

To reply to the message you're reading, click the **Reply** button. The **New Message** window opens with the text of the original message in the edit pane. If the message was sent to multiple addresses (as listed in the **To** and **Cc** text boxes), you can send your reply to all the addressees by clicking **Reply All** instead.

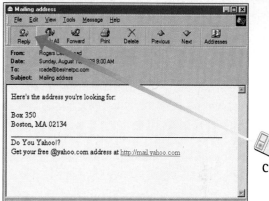

Click

6 Forward a Message

To send a copy of a message to another email address, click the **Forward** button. You can send the forwarded message without changes, or you can add your own comments to it. (You also can forward a message while viewing your **Inbox** list: Click the message and then click the **Forward** button.)

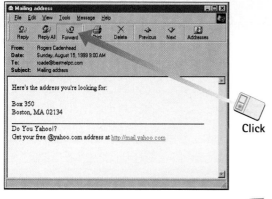

Click

End

TASK 4

How to Send an Attached File

Any file that's stored on your computer can be sent through email. Before the file can be opened by the recipient, however, it must be downloaded—transferred from the mail server to the recipient's computer. The amount of time this takes depends on the Internet connection speed and the file's size. A 200KB file takes more than 10 minutes to download at the most common Internet speed (28,800bps) and usually prevents the recipient from receiving other mail during the transfer. For this reason, you should send large files only to people who are expecting them.

Begin

1 Start Outlook Express

You send a file by attaching it to any email message you're sending out. Open Outlook Express (click the **Start** button and choose **Programs, Outlook Express**). Click the **new Mail message** hyperlink to begin writing a new message.

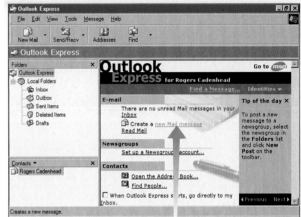

Click

2 Attach a File

After writing and addressing the message, click the **Attach** button in the toolbar at the top of the window. The **Insert Attachment** dialog box opens; you use this dialog box to locate the file that you want to attach to the message.

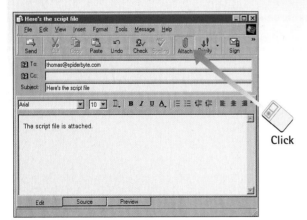

Click

3 Choose the File

Using standard Windows file-selection techniques, open the folder that contains the file you're going to send. Select the filename and then click the **Attach** button.

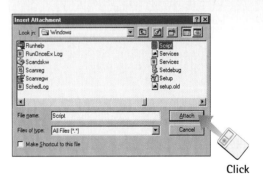

Click

4 Send the Email and Its Attachment

The name of the file you've chosen is displayed in the **Attach** text box at the top of the message window. Click the **Send** button to deliver the message and its attached file. The file is uploaded to your mail server, so the time it takes to send the message depends on the speed of your Internet connection and the size of the file.

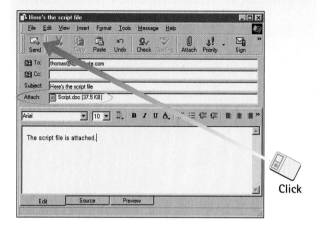

Click

5 Choose Multiple Files

You can attach more than one file to a message. In the message window, click the **Attach** button to open the **Insert Attachment** dialog box. If the files you want to send are in the same folder, hold the **Shift** key as you click the name of each file. When all the desired files are highlighted, click the **Attach** button.

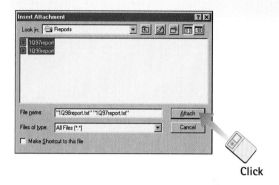

Click

6 Send the Files

The name of each attached file appears in the **Attach** text box of the message window. Click the **Attach** button again if you want to choose another file to attach to the message. Click **Send** to send the message and its attached files.

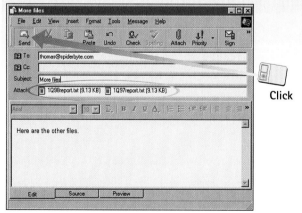

Click

How-To Hints

Sending a Shortcut Instead of a File

If you are sending an attached file to someone on the same *intranet*—computers networked together at a business, school, or other institution—you may be able to send a shortcut instead of the entire file. If the file you are sending is in a public folder on your intranet, open the **Insert Attachment** window, pick the file, and click the **Make a Shortcut to this file** box before clicking the **Attach** button.

End

How to Receive an Attached File

Files are delivered through Internet email by attaching them to normal email messages. To receive an attached file in Outlook Express, you must first open the message associated with the file. You can open files directly from Outlook Express or save them to a folder on your system. Attached files can contain viruses that execute damaging code on your computer—even in documents created with Microsoft Word. Although some antivirus programs can scan incoming files as they are received through email, you should be cautious before opening files sent to you.

2 Check for Attachments

Mail that has attached files is displayed with a paper clip icon. Open the mail message (click the message in the top-right pane to view it in the bottom-right pane). To open the file attached to the mail message, click the paper clip button and select the name of the file attached to the mail message.

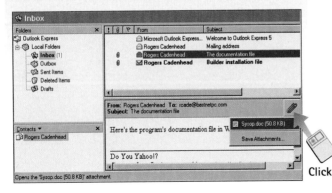

Click

Begin

1 Read Your Mail

Open Outlook Express (click the **Start** button and choose **Programs, Outlook Express**). If you have new mail, click the **unread Mail** hyperlink to open your Outlook Express **Inbox**.

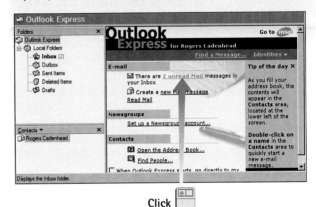

Click

3 Open the File

For security reasons (because files can contain viruses or code that can damage your system), Outlook Express warns you before opening an attached file. If you decide to open the file in Outlook Express, in the **Open Attachment** dialog box, click the **Open it** radio button and then click **OK**. The file is opened by the program associated with it (if there is one). If no program is associated with the file type, you'll be asked to pick a program that should open the file.

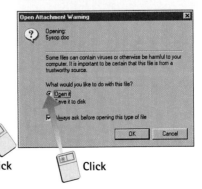

Click

4 Save an Attachment

To save an attached file to your system's hard drive instead of opening it in Outlook Express, click the paper clip button in the message window and choose **Save Attachments**. The **Save Attachments** dialog box opens.

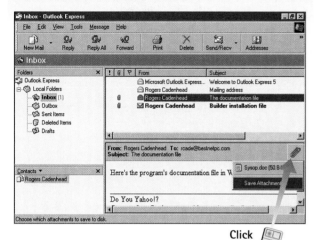

Click

5 Choose a Location

Click the **Browse** button next to the **Save To** text box to choose the folder in which you want to save the attached file. Then click the **Save** button.

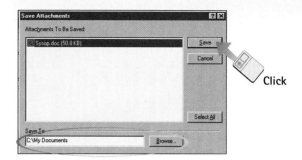

Click

6 View Attachments

When you're reading mail in a separate window, Outlook Express does not display a paper clip icon. Instead, the name of the attached file is displayed in the **Attach** text box at the top of the window. Double-click the filename to see the **Open Attachment** dialog box, which can be used to open or save the attached file.

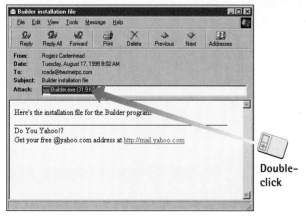

Double-click

How-To Hints

Protecting Yourself Against Damaging Email

File attachments are a major source of new computer viruses. If you open an attached file that contains a virus, the virus will run and may damage files on your computer. For this reason, you should not open an attached file unless you know who sent the file to you and are sure of its authenticity. If you run antivirus programs on your computer and keep them up to date, you should save attached files to disk and run a virus check on them before opening the files.

End

TASK 6

How to Find Someone's Email Address

Several sites on the World Wide Web (including Yahoo! and InfoSpace) offer huge directories of email addresses. If you want to contact a person, company, or other organization but don't know the contact's email address, you can use Outlook Express to search through each of these directories. You can use these same steps to quickly search your own *address book* (a personal database of your email correspondents you can create in Outlook Express).

Begin

1 Find People

To begin looking for the email address of a person or company in Outlook Express, click the arrow next to the **Find** button and select the **People** option. The **Find People** dialog box opens.

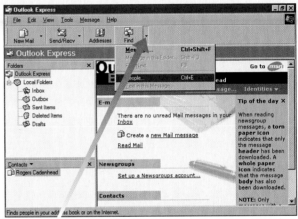

 Click

2 Search Your Address Book

To search through your personal address book in Outlook Express, choose **Address Book** from the **Look in** drop-down list at the top of the dialog box. Type the name you're looking for in at least one of the text boxes—**Name**, **E-mail**, **Address**, **Phone**, or **Other**. Click the **Find Now** button to start the search.

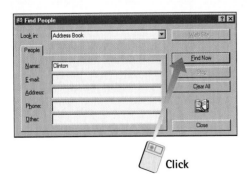

Click

3 Send Someone a Message

The **Find People** dialog box expands to display the results of the search. To begin a new email message addressed to one of the people you find, right-click the name and choose **Action**, **Send Mail** from the context menus that appear.

 Right-click

4 Search a Web Directory

You also can look for email addresses in several Web directories. In the **Find People** dialog box, in the **Look in** drop-down list, choose one of the directory services (for example, choose **Yahoo! People Search** or **InfoSpace**). Type the name you want to look for in the **Name** or **E-mail** text box and click the **Find Now** button.

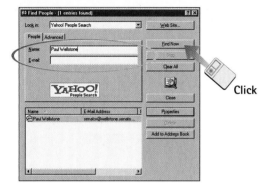
Click

5 Add to Your Address Book

If you find the person or company you are looking for, you can copy the information from the Web directory to your personal address book. Click the name in the results pane and then click the **Add to Address Book** button.

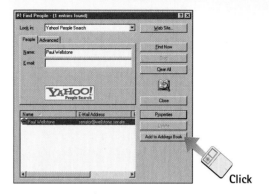
Click

6 Visit a Directory Site

Each of the address directories in Outlook Express has a related Web site that offers additional features and more sophisticated search tools. From the **Look in** list box, select the name of the directory you want to use and then click the **Web Site** button to visit a directory's site with your Web browser.

Click

End

How-To Hints

Adding Someone to Your Address Book

You can add people to your Outlook Express address book as you are reading a message from that person in its own window. Double-click the name or email address you want to add, then click the **Add to Address Book** button.

How to Subscribe to a Mailing List

A popular way to use email is to communicate with a group of people on a shared topic of interest. This is done by joining an *electronic mailing list*, a discussion that takes place entirely with email. People who are interested in a list's topic send an email message to subscribe. If the list allows public participation (as many do), you can use a special email address to send a message to all members. Any message sent by another member of the list of subscribers winds up in your Inbox.

Begin

1 Create a New Message

Before you can subscribe to a mailing list, you must know its subscription address and the command used to subscribe. When you have that information, begin a new email message in Outlook Express by clicking the **new Mail message** hyperlink.

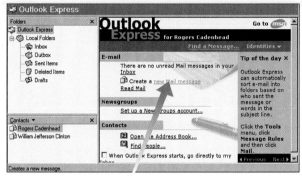

Click

2 Subscribe to a List

Address the message by typing the list's subscription address in the **To** text box. Type the subscription command in the body of the message or in the **Subject** text box—whichever the mailing list requires you to do. Note that subscription procedures for mailing lists are often very specific; type exactly *what* the mailing list tells you to type, exactly *where* it tells you to type it.

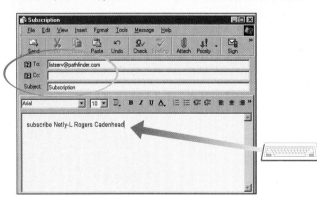

3 Send the Message

Click the **Send** button to deliver your subscription request. You'll receive a confirmation message when you have been added to the mailing list; the confirmation message usually contains helpful information about how to use the list.

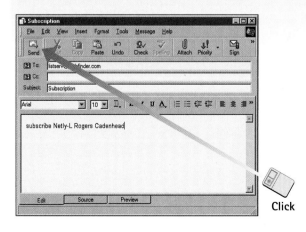
Click

4 Contribute to the List

If the mailing list allows public participation, you can send a message to all list members using a special email address. Usually, this address includes the name of the list—see your confirmation message for more information. Click **Send** to deliver the message.

This address is probably not the same as the address to which you subscribed.

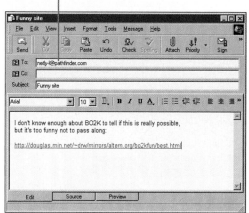

5 Unsubscribe from a List

When you subscribe to a mailing list, you should save the confirmation message you received. This message usually contains instructions on how to quit the list. The address to which you mail your request to be removed from the list is often the same as the one you used to subscribe, but the command will be slightly different. Click **Send** to deliver the request.

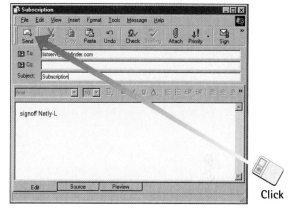

Click

End

How-To Hints

Finding Mailing Lists on Any Topic

There are thousands of mailing lists on topics related to technology, entertainment, hobbies, and many other things. To search a database of lists you can join, visit the Liszt World Wide Web site at **http://www.liszt.com**.

Joining the Netly-L Mailing List

One popular general-interest mailing list is Netly-L, a place to discuss the Internet, online media, and technology. To subscribe, send an email message to **listserv@pathfinder.com**. In the body of the message, type **subscribe Netly-L** followed by your name (for example, if your name is Ulysses S. Grant, type **subscribe Netly-L Ulysses S. Grant** in the body of the message).

How to Set Up a Free Web-Based Email Account

Although you receive an email account when you subscribe to most Internet service providers, you may want to set up an account with a World Wide Web site that provides free lifetime email. These sites normally offer mail that you access by visiting the site with your Web browser. However, some services can work in conjunction with Outlook Express and other mail software. An advantage of a Web-based mail account is that you can take it with you when you switch to a different Internet provider. In this task, you use Outlook Express to set up a free email account with Microsoft Hotmail.

How-To Hints

Choosing a Unique Hotmail Username

No two people on Hotmail have the same username, and there are already millions of people using this email service. For this reason, you may find it difficult to pick a unique username when you are signing up to use Hotmail. If your desired username is taken, one way to change it is to add a year or another number at the end—for example, **robotfood2000**.

Begin

1 Sign Up for a New Account

To get started, open Outlook Express (click the **Start** button and choose **Programs, Outlook Express**). From the menu bar at the top of the screen, select **Tools, New Account Signup, Hotmail**. Hotmail's terms and conditions of service are displayed.

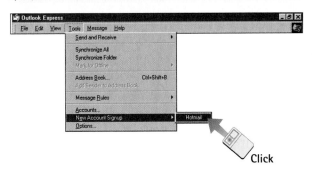
Click

2 Choose a Username

If you accept Hotmail's terms and conditions, you can begin setting up an account. Type your desired username, a password, and your name, then click the **Next** button to continue. (For tips on picking a unique username, see the How-To Hint on this page.

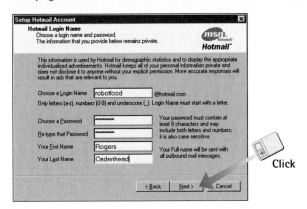
Click

3 Provide More Information

Use the **County/Region** drop-down list to identify your location, click the radio button for your gender, and type your year of birth. Click **Next** to continue.

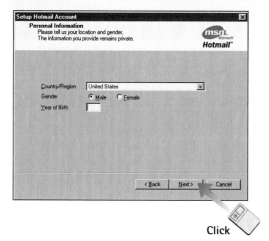

Click

4 Identify Your Time Zone

When you send email using Hotmail, your local time is used to set the time at which the message was delivered. From the **Time Zone** drop-down list, select your time zone and then provide additional information about your location. Click **Next** when you're done.

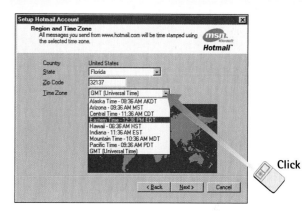

Click

5 Choose a Reminder

If you forget your Hotmail password, you can get it from the service by answering a personal reminder question such as *What is your mother's maiden name?* Type a question and its answer in the text boxes provided and click **Next** to continue.

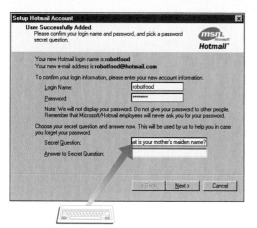

6 Pick WebCourier Services

Hotmail offers several free services through WebCourier, a feature that delivers information from Web sites to your Hotmail account. Place your mouse over the name of a service to find out more about it; check the box if you want to subscribe.

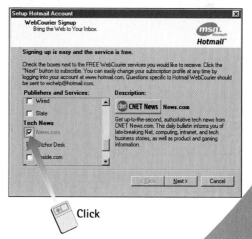

Click

End

How to Use Your Free Web-Based Email Account

The preceding task described how to set up a free Hotmail account with Outlook Express. After you've done this, Hotmail service is fully integrated into all the features of Outlook Express. You can send and receive email through your Hotmail account and any other accounts you have set up. Hotmail messages are stored in their own set of folders, separate from your other Outlook Express mail—in separate **Inbox**, **Sent Items**, and **Deleted Item** folders.

Begin

1 Check Your Hotmail Account

Start Outlook Express (click the **Start** button and choose **Programs**, **Outlook Express**). To see messages that have been sent to your Hotmail account, click the **Hotmail Inbox** folder in the top-left pane of the window.

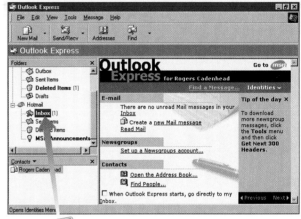

Click

2 Start a New Message

Start a new message with Hotmail: Click the **New Mail** button in the toolbar at the top of the screen. A new message window opens.

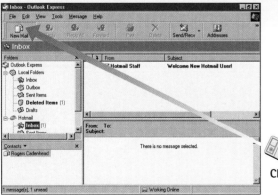

Click

3 Choose an Account

Click the arrow to the right of the **From** drop-down list and select the address the message should be sent from. (If you have only an Outlook Express email account, the **From** list box does not appear in the new message window.) The **From** list box contains your Hotmail account, your Outlook Express account, and any other email accounts you may have set up.

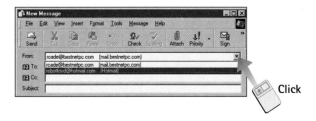

Click

4 Send the Message

After you have specified the recipient of your message in the **To** text box and typed the body of your message, click the **Send** button to deliver the message using Hotmail. If the recipient replies to the message, the reply is received in your **Hotmail Inbox** folder.

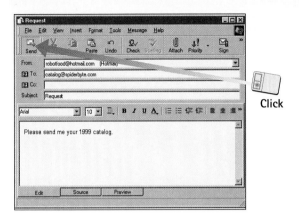

Click

5 Change Mail Settings

If you want Hotmail to be your default mail service, you can change your Outlook Express settings to make that happen. From the **Tools** menu, choose **Accounts**. The **Internet Accounts** dialog box opens.

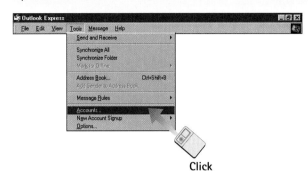

Click

6 Choose a Default

Click the **Mail** tab to bring that tabbed window to the front. All your mail accounts are listed. To make your Hotmail account the default, click the **Hotmail** list item and then click the **Set as Default** button.

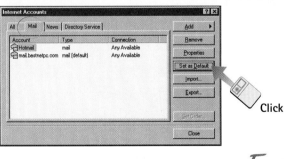

Click

End

How-To Hints

Using Hotmail as Your Public Email Address

One of the biggest annoyances for people who use email is the growing problem of *spam*—unsolicited commercial email that is sent to thousands of Internet users at the same time. This electronic junk mail often is sent to promote disreputable or obscene businesses. It can take a lot of your time and patience to read and delete these letters. You may want to use a Hotmail address as your public email address—the one you use on Web sites, Usenet, and other places where a spam sender might find it. Another email address, such as the one provided by your Internet service provider, can be your private email address—given only to friends, relatives, and business colleagues.

How to Print an Email Message

You can print email from Outlook Express using the standard Windows printing interface. Email can contain the same kind of content as a Web page (as long as your mail software supports that feature). For this reason, printing a message is similar to printing a Web page: You can print the current message, print all the hyperlinks it contains, and print a collection of linked pages. Messages can be sent to a printer, sent out using a fax modem, and saved as a disk file.

Begin

1 Choose the Print Command

To print the message you're currently reading in Outlook Express, choose **File**, **Print**. The **Print** dialog box opens.

Click

2 Choose a Printer

You can send email to any printer or fax modem that has been installed on your system. To select a printer, click the arrow to the right of the **Name** drop-down list and drag to select the correct device.

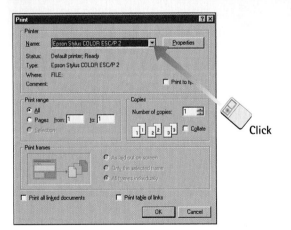

Click

3 Print Associated Web Pages

Outlook Express can look at any hyperlinks contained in the email and print the pages associated with those links. If you want to do this, select the **Print all linked documents** option.

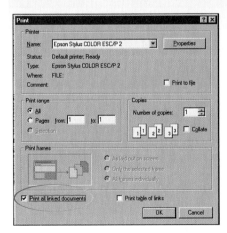

4 List All Hyperlinks

You also can print a list of all the hyperlinks contained in the email message. To obtain such a list, select the **Print table of links** option.

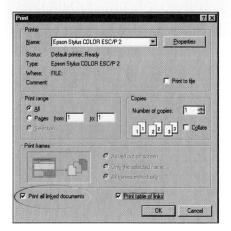

5 Print Multiple Copies

To print more than one copy of the message, click the spin-button arrows next to the **Number of copies** box. Click **OK** to close the **Print** dialog box and send the email message to the printer you selected.

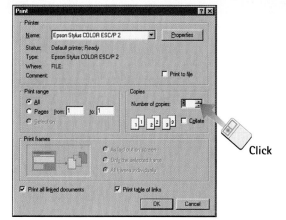

Click

End

How-To Hints

Dithering Graphics to Print Email Faster

To make the graphics in an email message easier and faster to print, you can use *dithering*, a process that reduces the number of colors in the graphic. In the **Print** dialog box, click the **Properties** button to display the **<printer> Properties** dialog box, where you can set your printer's properties. Click the **Graphics** tab and choose a new **Dithering** setting: **None, Coarse, Fine, Line Art**, or **Error Diffusion**. Click **OK** to close the **<printer> Properties** dialog box; click **OK** to close the **Print** dialog box and send the email message to the printer with the dithering option you specified.

Task

7

Participating in Usenet Discussion Groups

*O*ne of the most popular communities on the Internet is Usenet, a collection of public discussion groups on a diverse range of topics. Usenet groups, which also are called *newsgroups*, are distributed by thousands of Internet sites around the world.

Newsgroups function in a manner similar to electronic mailing lists (which were described in Part 6, Task 7, "How to Subscribe to a Mailing List"). Subscribers join a group they are interested in, read the messages written by other subscribers, and contribute their own messages. There's a big difference: Mailing lists are distributed by a single computer—thousands of computers distribute each Usenet message. When you post a message in a Usenet newsgroup, it is stored on the server you use. The message is then copied by all other servers connected to Usenet that carry the newsgroup.

The decentralized design of Usenet gives it a unique personality. Messages can't be removed from all those servers after they are sent. Although a small number of Usenet newsgroups have a moderator who must approve messages before they are distributed, most newsgroups are unrestricted. Unlike a Web site or a mailing list, no one can stop a discussion by taking control of the right computer. Usenet also is set up so that new discussion groups can be created quickly on any topic.

This freedom leads to many discussions that might never take place anywhere else but on Usenet. It also does little to discourage some things that shouldn't be taking place at all. ●

How to Set Up Outlook Express for Usenet Newsgroups

Outlook Express supports Usenet newsgroups in addition to email. To participate in Usenet, you must have access to a *news server*—an Internet site that can send and receive newsgroup messages. Many Internet service providers offer Usenet as part of a subscription—if yours does, the provider must give you the name of its news server. You also can subscribe to Usenet with services such as RemarQ and NewsGuy. Before you can set up Outlook Express to work with Usenet, you must have the name of your news server. If your server requires a username and password, you also must have these to get started.

How-To Hints

Subscribing to a Usenet Service

If your Internet service provider does not offer Usenet, you can subscribe to a Usenet news service. Charging about $9.95 per month, they usually offer more newsgroups than the free Usenet servers provided by ISPs. Visit the following Web sites to find out more:

✓ **RemarQ:** http://www.remarq.com

✓ **NewsGuy:** http://www.newsguy.com

Begin

1 Run Outlook Express

To get started, launch Outlook Express: Click the **Start** button and choose **Programs**, **Outlook Express**.

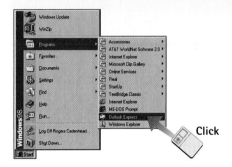

Click

2 Set Up Newsgroups

If Outlook Express has not already been set up to work with Usenet, a **Set up a Newsgroups account** hyperlink will be displayed. Click this hyperlink to start the **Internet Connection Wizard**.

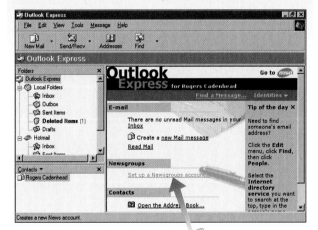

Click

3 Identify Yourself

A name will be displayed on all messages you post in Usenet newsgroups. In the **Display name** text box, type the name, or *handle*, that will identify you. Unlike email, where real names are the norm, on Usenet it is commonplace for people to use a handle, nickname, or similar pseudonym when posting messages. Click **Next** to continue.

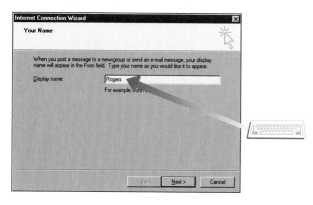

4 Identify Your Address

An email address also will be displayed on Usenet messages. In the **E-mail address** text box, type your email address and click **Next** to continue.

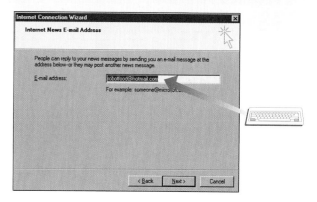

5 Identify Your Server

Type your server's name in the **News (NNTP) Server** text box. Most news servers do not require a username and password. If your server does not require you to log on, click **Next** to finish setting up your Usenet service. If your news server does require you to log on, check the **My news server requires me to log on** box. When you click **Next** to continue, you'll be asked for your username and password for the news server.

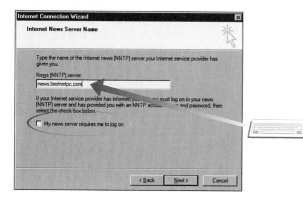

6 Set Up Usenet Service

After you have created a Usenet account, you are asked whether you want to download newsgroups from your server. These newsgroups are needed so that you can find discussion groups on topics of interest. Click the **Yes** button to download them.

Click

End

How to Read a Newsgroup

After you have set up Usenet service in Outlook Express, you're ready to read *news*—public messages contributed to the various newsgroups. There are more than 30,000 newsgroups on many Usenet servers, and some of the more popular groups receive more than 100 messages a day. If you find a newsgroup you'd like to read on a regular basis, you can subscribe to it and keep up with the group more easily.

Begin

1 Read Usenet Messages

To begin reading newsgroups in Outlook Express, launch Outlook Express as described in Task 1 of this part. Click the **Read News** hyperlink.

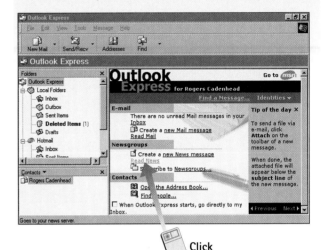

Click

2 View Newsgroups

If you have not subscribed to any newsgroups, you'll be asked whether you want to see a list of available groups. Click the **Yes** button to display the Newsgroup Subscriptions dialog box. (If you have subscribed to any groups, you can view available groups by clicking the **Newsgroups** button in the news window when it opens.)

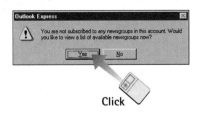

Click

3 Search Newsgroups

Usenet newsgroups are given names that describe their purpose. To search for groups on a topic, type the topic in the **Display newsgroups which contain** text box. As you type, matching groups will be listed in the bottom pane of the window.

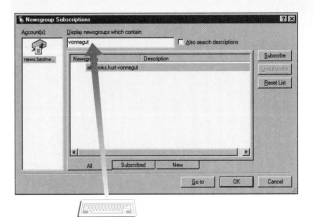

4 Choose a Group

If you want to read the messages in one of the newsgroups that are listed as a result of your search term, click the newsgroup name and then click the **Go to** button.

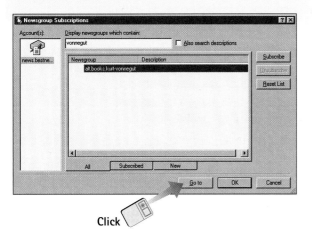

Click

5 Read Messages

Outlook Express displays Usenet messages similarly to the way it displays email. Click the subject of a message to view that message; double-click the subject to view the message in a new window.

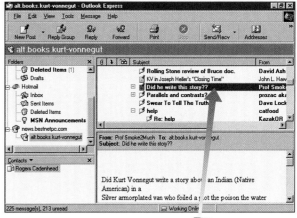

Click

6 Subscribe to a Group

The easiest way to read Usenet newsgroups is to subscribe to the groups you frequent. To subscribe to a group while reading it, right-click the group name in the **Folders** pane and select **Subscribe** from the context menu that appears. The next task explains how to read news for newgroups you've subscribed to.

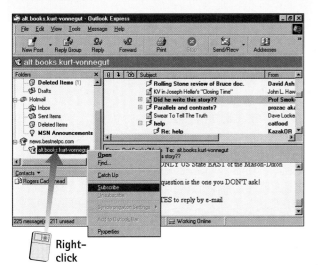

Right-click

How-To Hints

Finding Groups by Their Descriptions

Many newsgroups also have brief descriptions that provide more information about the group. To search through these descriptions as you're looking for newsgroups, click the **Also search descriptions** check box in Step 4. Descriptions must be downloaded the first time you use this option.

End

How to Read Newsgroups You Have Subscribed To

The most convenient way to read Usenet newsgroups in Outlook Express is to subscribe to them. The preceding task explained how to subscribe to a newsgroup with Outlook Express. The software keeps track of your subscription internally and makes it easy to follow new discussions. After you have subscribed to a group, you can automatically download new subjects and messages with the synchronization feature. One thing to note about Usenet subscriptions is that mailing lists you subscribe to are private. Although some electronic *mailing lists* have public subscriber lists, there are no public lists of people who have subscribed to a Usenet newsgroup.

How-To Hints

Stop Retrieving Messages from a Subscribed Group

If you want to put a Usenet subscription on hold for a while, choose the group, click the **Settings** button, and choose **Don't Synchronize**. You'll remain subscribed, but you won't retrieve any messages or subject headings until you change the **Settings** option for that group.

Begin

1 View Newsgroups

After you have subscribed to a newsgroup you want to read, you can read the news for that group at any time. Open Outlook Express and click the **Read News** hyperlink to begin setting up synchronization. A new window opens; Outlook Express uses the name of your news server as the window's title when you read news.

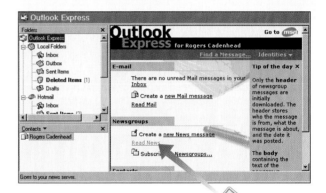

Click

2 Set Up Newsgroups

Synchronization determines how a subscribed newsgroup will be updated. To set up a group so that new subject headings are downloaded, click the name of the newsgroup in the right pane of the window, click the **Settings** button, and then choose **Headers Only** from the drop-down list.

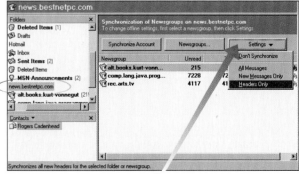

Click

3 Download All Messages

To set up a group so that all messages are downloaded automatically to a Usenet folder in Outlook Express, click the group name, click the **Settings** button, and then choose **All Messages**. This is the most time consuming (and disk space–consuming) option, especially for a popular group.

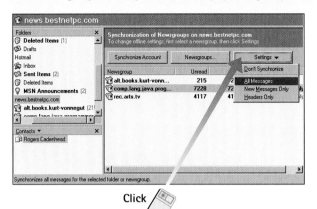

Click

4 Download New Messages

To set up a group so that new messages are downloaded as they arrive, click the group name, click the **Settings** button, and then choose **New Messages Only**.

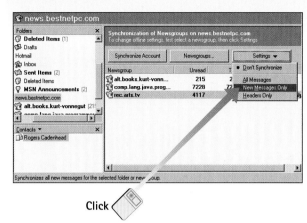

Click

5 Synchronize Newsgroups

After you have specified how you want to synchronize your newsgroups, click the **Synchronize Account** button to retrieve messages based on the settings specified in the **Synchronization Settings** column. Click this button every time you want to check your server for new Usenet messages in your subscribed groups.

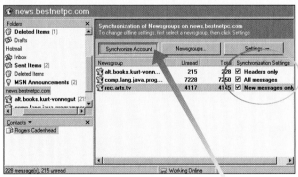

Click

6 Retrieve Messages

As Outlook is synchronizing newsgroups and downloading any messages, it displays a progress dialog box. Click the **Details** button to see more information on what Outlook Express is retrieving.

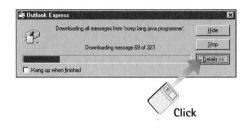

Click

End

How to Post a Message to a Newsgroup

Anyone who reads a Usenet newsgroup can participate in its discussions by posting his or her own messages. Your message may be distributed to thousands of servers around the world, depending on the newsgroups you're posting to. One thing you'll become acquainted with as you post messages is the concept of *netiquette*—commonly accepted standards for behavior on the Internet. Although you *can* post a Usenet message to as many groups as you like, established netiquette says you *should* post to four groups or less.

Begin

1 Post a New Message

After you have decided which newsgroup(s) you want to post a message to, click the **new News message** hyperlink in Outlook Express. A **New Message** dialog box opens.

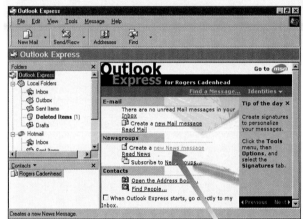

Click

2 Choose Newsgroups

In the **Newsgroups** text box, type the name of the group to which you want to post this message. You can specify more than one newsgroup if you separate the group names with commas.

3 Send a Copy by Mail

You also can email a copy of your newsgroup posting to anyone who has an Internet email account—regardless of whether that person reads the newsgroup you're posting to. Type the recipient's email address in the **Cc** text box.

4 Describe Your Message

In the **Subject** text box, type a succinct description of your message. The subject helps Usenet news readers skim a Usenet newsgroup looking for topics that interest them.

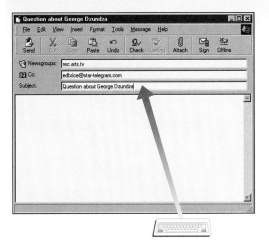

5 Send Your Message

Type the text of the message you want to post, then click the **Send** button. Your message will be submitted to the newsgroup on your news server and distributed to servers around the world.

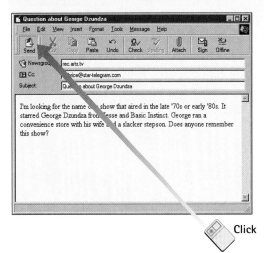

Click

6 Reply to a Message

You also can post messages on Usenet by replying to the message you're reading. With the message selected and displayed in the right pane, click the **Reply Group** button. A modified **New Message** window opens. (If you want to reply by email to the author of a Usenet message rather than replying to a newsgroup, click the **Reply** button.)

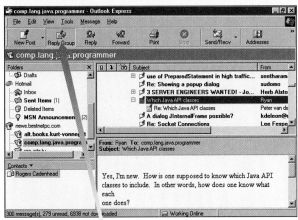

Click

7 Send Your Reply

The text of your reply starts out with the name of the newsgroup you're responding to in the **Newsgroups** box, the **Subject** line filled in (with Re: prefixed to the subject line of the original message), and the text of the original message. If the original message is lengthy, good netiquette dictates that you delete most of this text, leaving only enough to make it clear what you're replying to. Type your reply and click the **Send** button to distribute the message to the newsgroup.

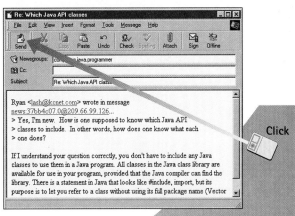

Click

End

How to Find a Newsgroup

As you're searching for newsgroups in Outlook Express, you may be dismayed to find no groups devoted to a topic you're interested in. There's a chance that you can find a relevant newsgroup elsewhere—no single Usenet server carries all newsgroups. Currently, there are more than 40,000 Usenet newsgroups; more than a dozen new ones are created every day. After you've searched for a group using Outlook Express, you can use sites on the World Wide Web such as Liszt and Deja.Com to find other newsgroups.

Begin

1 Search in Outlook

Start by looking for newsgroups in Outlook Express. Open Outlook Express and click the **Newsgroups** hyperlink. The **Newsgroup Subscriptions** dialog box opens.

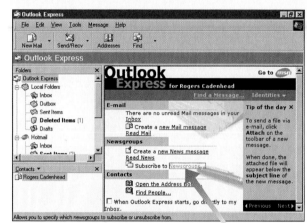

Click

2 Search for Newsgroup Names

To search for specific text in a newsgroup name, type the text in the **Display newsgroups which contain** text box. Outlook Express displays results as you're entering text. To subscribe to a group, click its name, then click the **Subscribe** button.

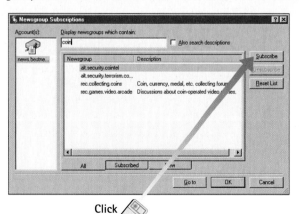

Click

3 Search Descriptions

To search for text in names and descriptions, check the **Also search descriptions** box. The first time you select this option, descriptions are downloaded from your Usenet server to your local machine to speed up the search process.

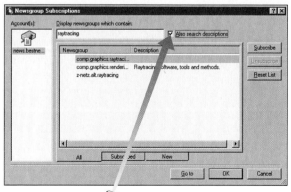

 Click

4 Find Other Groups

Several World Wide Web sites offer directories of Usenet groups. To use the Liszt directory, launch your Web browser, type the URL **http://www.liszt.com/news** in the browser's Address bar, and press **Enter**.

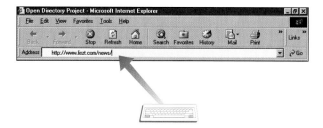

5 Search the Directory

When the Liszt home page opens, click the **Usenet Newsgroups** radio button, type the text you're looking for in the search box, and click the **Go** button.

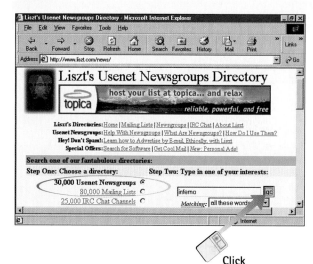

Click

6 Read Newsgroups

If Liszt finds any groups that match the text you typed, you can read them in two different ways. Click the **local** hyperlink to read the group within Outlook Express (if it can be found on your Usenet server). If the **local** hyperlink is not available (or if you want to read news from a different server), click the newsgroup's name to read it on Deja.Com, a Web site that offers newsgroup access.

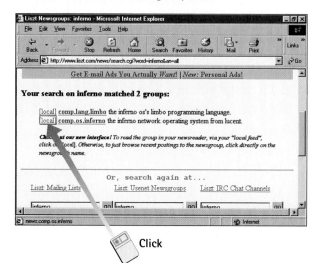

Click

How-To Hints

Comparing Your Usenet Server to Others

One of the best reasons to use a Web directory of Usenet newsgroups is because many groups will be completely unknown to you. No Usenet server offers a full assortment of the more than 40,000 newsgroups currently available, and many servers carry only those groups that have been specifically requested by users. Deja.Com is available on the World Wide Web at **http://www.deja.com**. For more information on how to search Deja.Com for newsgroups and other information, see the next task, "How to Search an Archive of Past Newsgroup Discussions."

End

How to Search an Archive of Past Newsgroup Discussions

An important thing to note about Usenet is that it's routinely archived. Messages you post to newsgroups are archived by several Web sites, and those archives can be searched by topic and by author. The most popular archive, Deja.Com, has Usenet discussions that date back to late 1995. This archive is a good place to find newsgroups you aren't familiar with because Deja.Com has one of the largest collections of Usenet newsgroups. Deja.Com is also a great research tool on many subjects—especially technical subjects related to the Internet and computers.

How-To Hints

More About Deja.Com

Because Deja.Com has the most comprehensive archive of Usenet discussions, it's a convenient place to read newsgroups not available on your Usenet server. Load the Web site's home page and click the **My Deja** hyperlink.

All the Usenet messages you post are archived by Deja.Com—if its server receives them. To keep a message out of the archive, type the text **X-No-Archive: Yes** on a line of its own in the body of your message.

Begin

1 Visit Deja.Com

To visit the Deja.Com home page, start your Web browser, type the URL **http://www.deja.com** into the Address bar, and press **Enter**. The Web page opens in your browser window.

2 Choose an Archive

The Quick Search section of the Deja.Com home page can be used to search its archive of Usenet messages. Click the **Discussions** hyperlink to indicate that you will be searching Usenet newsgroup discussions.

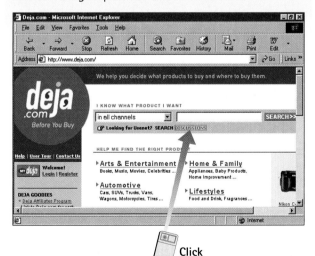

Click

3 Search the Archive

Type the text you're looking for in the search box and click **Search** to begin a search.

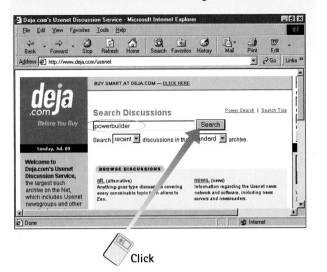

Click

4 Read Messages

In the results list, Deja.Com lists the headings and newsgroups of the messages that turn up in its archive. To read a message, click the appropriate hyperlink in the **Subject** column.

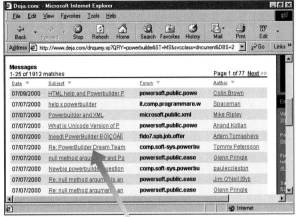

Click

5 Power Search the Archive

For a more advanced search, return to the Deja.Com Discussions page and click the **Power Search** hyperlink next to the **Search** button.

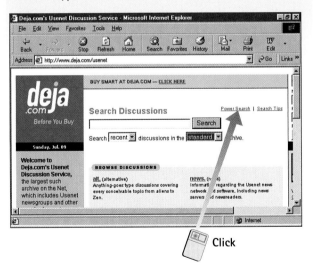

Click

6 Conduct a Search

The Power Search feature supports some common searching techniques. Place quotation marks around a specific phrase you're looking for, and use the AND keyword to find messages containing more than one keyword. Type your search text in the **Enter Keywords** box and click the **Search** button.

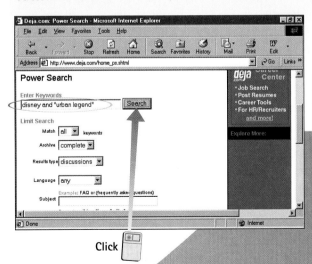

Click

End

How Not to Increase the Junk Email You Receive

When you start contributing to Usenet, you can count on receiving more email as a result. Unfortunately, a lot of this mail will be spam. Marketers who rely on spam to promote their products often build their mailing lists by scanning Usenet messages. You can deter this effort by posting with a fake email address. Your real address can be placed in a *signature file*—text that is automatically appended to email, Usenet postings, and similar documents.

Begin

1 Set Up Options

Start by creating a signature file in Outlook Express: From any screen in Outlook Express, pull down the **Tools** menu and select the **Options** command. The **Options** dialog box opens.

Click

2 Create a Signature

Click the **Signatures** tab to bring that page to the front of the dialog box. Click the **New** button to create a new signature file. The default signature filename (Signature #1) appears in the **Signatures** list box.

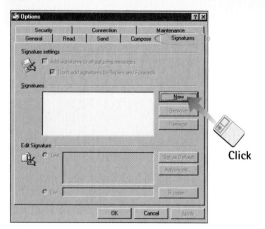

Click

3 Edit the Text

A signature file usually contains your name, email address, personal Web site, and similar personal information. In the **Text** box at the bottom of the dialog box, type the text for your signature file—including your real email address—and click the **Advanced** button. The **Advanced Signature Settings** dialog box opens.

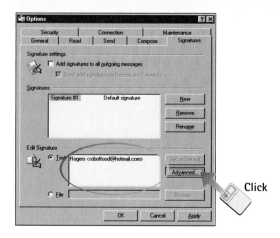

Click

4 Use a Signature

In the list box, select the check box in front of the Usenet account you want to use your new signature file with. If you want to use the signature file with other Outlook Express accounts, check those boxes also. Then click the **OK** button. Close the **Options** dialog box by clicking the **OK** button.

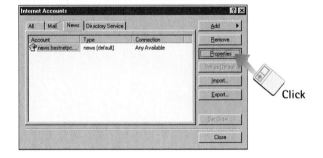

Click

5 Change Your Address

After creating a signature file, you should remove your real email address from your Usenet account. To do so, choose **Tools**, **Accounts** to open the **Internet Accounts** dialog box.

Click

6 Adjust Your Account

Click the **News** tab to view your Usenet newsgroup accounts. Select the account you want to change and then click the **Properties** button. The **<account> Properties** dialog box opens.

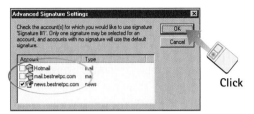

Click

7 Falsify Your Address

In the **E-mail address** text box on the **General** tab, type an obviously false email address (the address **see_my_sig@fakeaddress.com** is suitable for this purpose). Click **OK**. Usenet participants who want to send you mail will know to look for a signature if they want to contact you personally. Spammers will add the fake address to their mailing lists, and you'll never get unsolicited mail from vendors who picked up your email address from the newsgroup.

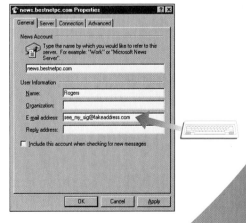

End

Task

8

Chatting Using Instant Messages with ICQ

*T*he most immediate way to communicate with someone over the Internet is by using *chat*—live, back-and-forth discussions between two or more people.

There are more than a dozen different ways to chat, including America Online's member-only chat rooms and World Wide Web chat pages. You also can use software equipped for Internet Relay Chat (IRC) or one of the new, free instant-messaging services offered by AOL, Microsoft, and others.

Instant-messaging is a style of chat in which you can keep track of people you know who are using the same software. A server tells you when selected people are online and provides the same information about you to others. You can send private messages that are received instantly on another user's computer.

The software that pioneered this style of communication is ICQ, a program named for the phrase *I Seek You*. An estimated 40 million people have downloaded ICQ's free software, making it the most popular instant-messaging service on the Internet. ●

How to Download ICQ

Before you can use ICQ, you must download and install the program on your computer. The software, which was developed by a company that has been purchased by America Online, is free. You can find copies of ICQ in several popular file archives, such as Download.com. To make sure that you install the current version of the software, visit the ICQ World Wide Web site, which will direct you to the places where ICQ's most up-to-date software can be downloaded.

Begin

1 Run Internet Explorer

To get started, double-click the **Internet Explorer icon** on your desktop. Internet Explorer launches and opens to your home page.

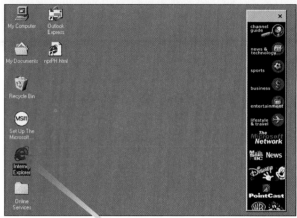

Double-click

2 Visit the ICQ Site

To visit the official ICQ Web site, type the URL **http://www.web.icq.com** in the Address bar and press the **Enter** key. The ICQ home page opens in the browser window.

3 View the Download Page

Read through the information on the ICQ home page to learn more about this program. Click the **Download ICQ** hyperlink when you are ready to start to download the program. The ICQ download page opens.

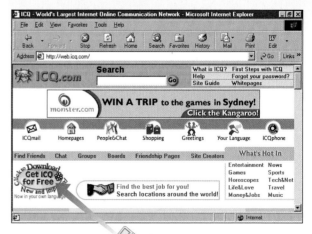

Click

4 Choose a Download Site

The ICQ site lists file archives that offer the current version of the software. Click the hyperlink associated with one of these places, such as **CNET Downloads**. There's usually no difference in download speed between the different sites, so you can pick the site you are most familiar with.

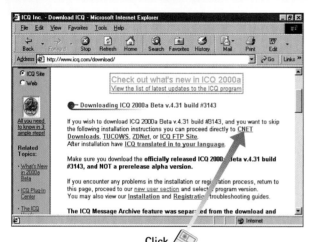

Click

5 Download the File

Each of the sites offers a hyperlink you can click to begin downloading ICQ. On the CNET Download.com site, click the **Download Now** hyperlink. The **File Download** dialog box opens.

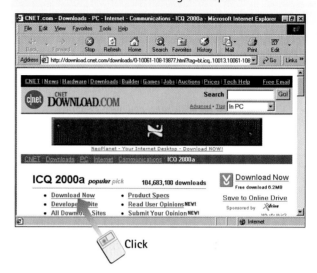

Click

6 Install Immediately

To begin installing the file as soon as the download is complete, check the **Run this program from its current location** option. Refer to Task 2, "How to Install ICQ," for instructions for running the program over the Internet.

Click

7 Save the ICQ Installation File to Disk

If you don't want to install ICQ immediately, check the **Save this program to disk** option in the **File Download** dialog box. Click **OK**. After the file is saved, begin installation by double-clicking its icon.

Click

End

How to Install ICQ

The current version of ICQ is available for free download over the Internet. The preceding task explained how to download the software by visiting the ICQ World Wide Web site. After you download the installation program, you can set up ICQ in two ways: by running it from the Internet or by saving the ICQ file to a folder on your system and then double-clicking its icon to launch the program. The program is available in English and non-English versions.

2 Close Other Programs

Without disconnecting from the Internet, close your Web browser and any other programs open on your system. From the **Welcome** screen of the installation program, click the **Next** button to continue.

Click

Begin

1 Begin Installation

If you are running the ICQ setup program directly from the Internet, click the **Yes** button when you see the confirmation dialog box shown here. Otherwise, find the folder where you downloaded the ICQ installation program and double-click its icon to begin installation. You'll be presented with the ICQ license agreement; if you agree to its terms, installation can begin.

Click

3 Choose a Folder

The setup program suggests the **Program Files\ICQ** folder as the place to install ICQ. You can accept this suggestion or navigate to another folder. When you've picked a folder, click the **Next** button.

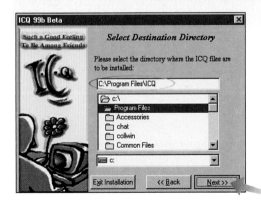

Click

4 Add to Start Menu

ICQ can install a shortcut icon in your Windows **Start** menu. If you want a shortcut icon there, select the **Yes** radio button and click **Next** to continue.

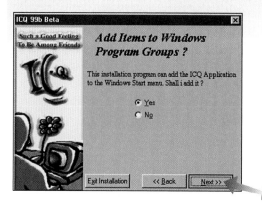

Click

5 Choose a Programs Folder

Setup suggests that a new ICQ folder be created for the program's shortcuts. To pick an existing folder, click the folder name in the list box. Alternatively, type a new folder name in the text box. Click **Next** to go on.

Click

6 Choose a Language

Select the radio button associated with the language you use on your machine and click **Next**.

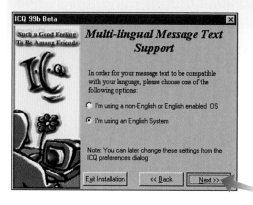

Click

7 Check Old Versions

ICQ uses a database file to handle different tasks. The setup program makes sure that there are no incompatible ICQ databases on your system. Click the **OK** button to finish installing the software.

Click

End

How to Set Up a New ICQ Account

When you run ICQ for the first time, you'll be able to set up a free account with the service by answering questions about yourself. A few of the questions (such as your email address) are mandatory. Most of the questions are optional and relate to your personal interests, mailing address, telephone number, and the like. The information you provide can be used by other ICQ users who are looking for people with common interests.

Begin

1 Run the Software

Click the **Start** button and choose the **Programs** folder. Then select the folder containing the ICQ program. Finally, click the **ICQ** menu item to run the software. The first time you run the software, the **Registration Wizard** opens.

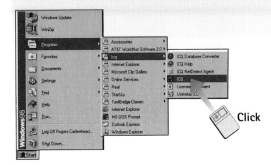

Click

2 Set Up a New Account

Select the **New ICQ#** radio button to set up an ICQ account for the first time. If you have established an account previously, click the **Existing ICQ#** radio button to provide your account information. Click **Next** to continue.

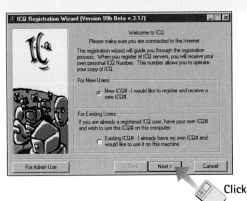

Click

3 Identify Your Connection

Select the radio button next to the option that describes your Internet connection. Click **Next** to continue.

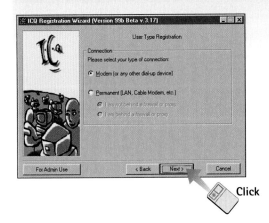

Click

4 Identify Yourself

Type your nickname, name, and email address in the appropriate text boxes. If you want ICQ to keep your email address private, select the **Don't publish my email address** option. Click **Next** to continue.

Click

5 Tell ICQ About Yourself

If you want to provide more information about yourself for ICQ's public database, fill out the text boxes on the next window that appears. Click buttons to provide more details on different subjects, such as your personal interests and home page address. Click **Next** to continue.

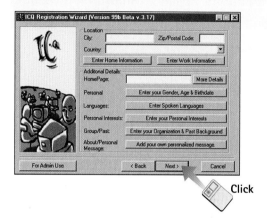

Click

6 Choose a Password

Type the password you want to use in the **Password** and **Confirm Password** text boxes. If you want to keep private the information about where you connected to the Internet, select the **Do not publish IP address** check box. Choose other options for your account and click **Next** to continue.

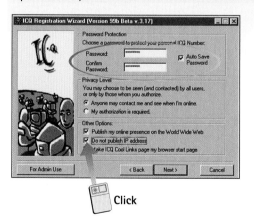

Click

7 Identify Your Mail Server

Choose your mail server from the list box and click **Next** to continue. Your ICQ account will be set up, and some tips for new users will be displayed in a dialog box. Click **Done** to start using ICQ.

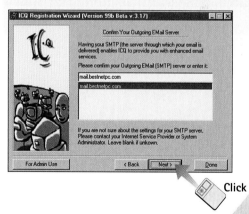

Click

End

How to Add Someone to Your Contact List

ICQ, like your Internet connection, adds its icon to the system tray—the area of the Windows taskbar closest to the current time. (The system tray is also called the status area.) You can display ICQ's main window by double-clicking the icon in the system tray. One of the ways to use ICQ is to keep in touch with people you know who are also ICQ users. You can track whether your friends are on ICQ by adding them to your contact list.

Begin

1 Load ICQ

If the ICQ icon is not visible in your system tray, click the **Start** button, choose the **Programs** folder, select the folder containing ICQ, and click the **ICQ** option. The ICQ icon appears in your system tray.

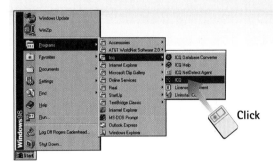

Click

2 Display the Menu

When you run the program, its icon is added to the system tray. Double-click this icon to open the program's main window.

Double-click

3 Add ICQ Users

To look for people you know in the ICQ database of users, click the **Add Users** button. The **Find/Add Users to Your List** dialog box opens.

Click

4 Begin a Search

You can search for an ICQ user by looking for an email address, a nickname, a first name, or a last name (or any combination of these items). Type text into at least one of the text boxes and click the corresponding **Search** button. ICQ searches its database and displays results at the bottom of the window.

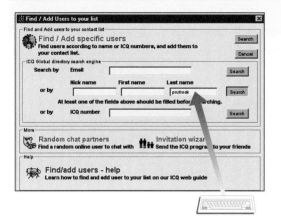

5 Add a Person

To make it easier for you to send ICQ messages to people you know, you can add them to your *contact list*—a menu of the people you communicate with most often. To add someone to your contact list from the search results list, click the person's ICQ number.

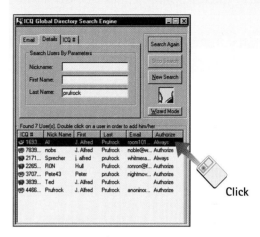

Click

6 Inspect a User

To find out more about a person in the list, right-click the person's ICQ number and select **User's Details** from the context menu that opens.

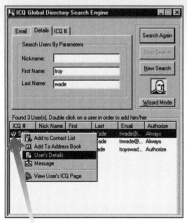

 Right-click

7 Delete a User

Everyone in your contact list is displayed in the main ICQ window. To remove someone from your list, click that person's name and choose **Delete** from the context menu.

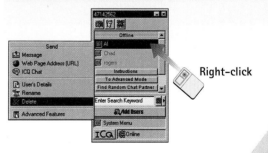

Right-click

End

How to Send Someone a Private Message

After you have added some people to your contact list, you can use ICQ to send private messages to them. Messages are delivered instantly if the person is connected to ICQ. Two things happen when new messages arrive: A distinctive sound is played, and the ICQ icon in the system tray changes. If the recipient isn't connected to ICQ, the message is delivered when he or she next makes a connection.

Begin

1 Run ICQ

If the ICQ icon is not visible in your system tray, click the **Start** button, choose the **Programs** folder, choose the folder containing ICQ, and click the **ICQ** menu item.

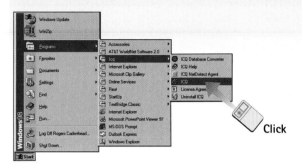

Click

2 Display the ICQ Menu

Double-click the **ICQ** icon in your system tray to open the program's main window.

Double-click

3 Choose a Contact

To send a private message to someone in your contact list, double-click the person's name in the ICQ main window. The **Send** window opens.

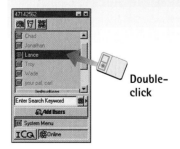

Double-click

4 Send a Message

Type the text of the message in the **Enter Message** text box, then click the **Send** button. If the recipient is connected to ICQ, your message is delivered immediately. Otherwise, the message will arrive when the person next connects to ICQ.

5 Reply to a Message

Incoming messages cause the ICQ icon in the system tray to change to an exclamation point. Click the icon to read the new message you have received. You can also send private messages in reply to the ones you receive. When you receive a message, the **Incoming Message** window opens so that you can read the note. To reply to the author of the message, click the **Reply** button. The **Send Online** Message window opens.

Click

6 Send Your Reply

Type the text of your reply in the **Enter Message** text box, then click **Send** to deliver the note.

Click

End

How to Join an Active List

As you know, ICQ helps you keep in touch with people you know by maintaining a contact list. If you want to communicate with people about a shared topic of interest, you can join an ICQ active list devoted to that topic. Active lists are similar to electronic mailing lists. Messages from the list arrive like any other ICQ message, but comments you send in reply are broadcast to every list member who is currently connected to ICQ. Active lists provide a form of chat that's unique to the service.

Begin

1 View Active Lists

Launch the ICQ main window by double-clicking the icon in the system tray or by selecting the program from the **Start** menu and then double-clicking the ICQ icon in the system tray. Click the **AL** (Active List) button in the toolbar at the top of the ICQ main window.

Click

2 Find a List

The ICQ main window changes to include buttons for Active List options. Click the **Find/Add An ICQ ActiveList** button. The ICQ **ActiveList Search Wizard** opens.

Click

3 Search Active Lists

To search for lists on topics of interest, select the **Search by Category** radio button and click **Next**. In the next window of the wizard, click the **Press to Edit Topic/Keywords** button.

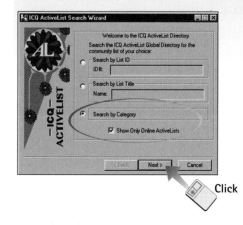

Click

4 Choose a Topic

To search for active lists related to a topic, select a topic from the list at the left side of the dialog box and click the **Add** button. The topic name appears in the **Selected Interests** list on the right side of the dialog box. Click **OK** to save your list of search topics. On the window that opens, click **Next** to start the search.

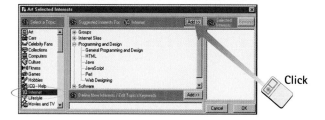

Click

5 Select a List

The results of the search are displayed in the wizard window. Click a list's name and then click the **More List's Info** button to find out more about that list. To join an active list, select the list name you want to join and click the **Next** button. You can request membership in that list or opt to view it as a guest. The list name is added to the **Member In** or **Guest In** area of the ICQ main window.

Click

6 Broadcast a Message

Messages you sent to an active list are broadcast to all list members who are currently online. To send a broadcast, double-click the list's name in the **Member In** area of the ICQ main window. The **Broadcast Message** window opens. Type your message in the **Enter Message** box and click **Broadcast** to send your message.

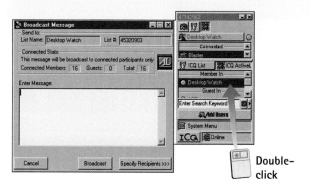

Double-
click

7 Close Active Lists

To close the display of active lists and see your normal contact list again, click the **AL** button in the toolbar at the top of the ICQ main window.

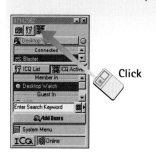

Click

End

Task

Using America Online's Internet Capabilities

*A*merica Online is the world's most successful online service, providing Internet access and other features to millions of people.

Like many other online services launched in the 1980s before the popularization of the Internet, America Online takes a more hands-on approach than most Internet service providers today. Instead of selling a connection to the Internet and letting you set up your own email, instant messaging, and chat software, America Online integrates these services into its own software. For this reason, America Online is marketed as a simpler service for new Internet users.

America Online offers access to the World Wide Web through a version of Internet Explorer that is integrated into the service. You also can run other Web browsers while connected to America Online.

There are two ways to connect to the service: by using your modem to dial up a local America Online access number or by using another Internet service provider's connection. The latter approach requires a secondary account with the other Internet provider, but your America Online subscription is discounted. ●

How to Install America Online for Windows

After turning on your computer, the basic installation procedure for AOL is simple. If you're running Windows, you may be able to use the version of America Online that's provided (it might not be the latest and greatest edition) and install it by following the onscreen instructions. If you're using an installation CD, the procedure will be a little bit different; see the How-To Hints for details. Depending on the speed of your computer, the entire process should take just a few minutes. You can also grab the software from AOL's site (use the keyword **Upgrade**), which ensures you of getting the most recent version—but it may take a fair amount of time to download.

Begin

1 Choose America Online

Before starting the installation process, close any applications that you are currently using. Then open the **Online Services** folder on your desktop and double-click **America Online**. (If single-click mode is on, you can click just once instead.) If you can't find the **Online Services** folder, open the **Start** menu, choose **Programs**, choose **Online Services**, and then choose **America Online**.

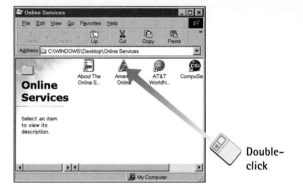

Double-click

3 Choose Installation Options

After a moment, the America Online installation program starts and opens a **Welcome to America Online** dialog box. In the next several windows, select the item that best describes your AOL situation and click **Next**. (If you select **Current Member** rather than **New Member**, as shown here, you'll see a slightly different set of prompts than what you see here.)

2 Choose the Appropriate Version

When the AOL **Welcome** screen opens, click the button for the appropriate version of America Online. For example, I need to use the United States version.

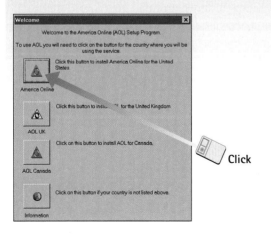

Click

4 Choose a Directory

This screen indicates where the AOL software will be installed. The default directory is **C:\America Online 5.0**. It's best to go with the default unless you have a good reason not to. (If you want to install AOL somewhere else, click the **Expert Install** button and choose a different directory.) Then click **Next**.

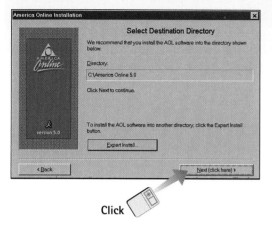

Click

5 Install AOL

AOL begins to install itself. The progress indicator in the **Installing** dialog box shows the progress of your installation; in addition, AOL displays some informational messages on the screen. (If for some reason you decide to cancel the installation, you can click the **Cancel** button. If you do this, however, you'll have to restart the installation from scratch.) The installation should go fairly quickly, and then you'll be ready to complete some easy setup steps, as described in the next task.

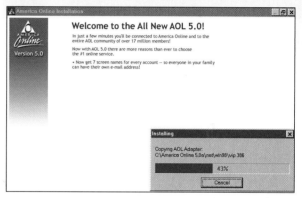

End

How-To Hints

Installing from Disk

To install AOL from disk, first insert your AOL 5 installation disk in the appropriate drive. If you're installing from a CD-ROM, the installation program should launch automatically. You should see the Welcome window shown in Step 3.

Understanding Drive Letters

If you're installing from disk, you need to know the drive letter of the disk drive you're using to install AOL for Windows. If you're using a CD-ROM, check in **My Computer** on your Windows desktop. The CD-ROM drive is represented by a CD-ROM disk icon. The icon is labeled with the drive letter—usually drive D or E.

How to Send Mail

Composing and sending email (or *mail*) to other AOL members and Internet users is easy. You type a message just as you would to send it by traditional mail, but instead of going through the bother of printing the message, addressing an envelope, and running down to the corner mailbox, you just click a few onscreen buttons. You don't even have to find or lick any stamps. Better yet, the price is the same whether you're sending your message down the hallway or around the world.

Begin

1 Choose the Write Icon

Make sure that you're signed on to AOL. Click the **Write** icon on the toolbar. (You can also press **Ctrl+M** or choose **Write Mail** from the **Mail Center** menu.) The **Write Mail** window opens. Incidentally, you can also compose email messages while you're offline and send them later—a great strategy if you want to minimize your time online.

Click

2 Enter a Screen Name or Email Address

In the **Send To** list box, type the recipient's screen name or Internet mail address. (If you want to type several addresses, separate them with commas.) It doesn't matter if you type the address in uppercase, lowercase, or a mixture of the two.

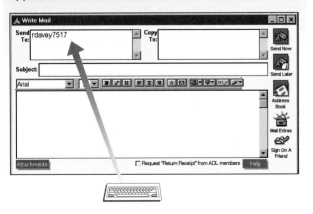

3 Send Carbon Copies

If you want to send a *carbon copy* of your message to another person, type his or her address in the **Copy To** list box. (To specify several recipients, separate their email addresses with commas.) To send a *blind carbon copy*, type the address in the **Copy To** list box and enclose it within parentheses. (Other recipients of the message won't be able to see that this person also received the message.)

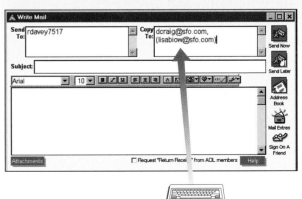

4 Type a Subject and Message

Type a subject for your message in the **Subject** box. Your recipients see this text before opening your message, so it's best to make the subject concise and descriptive. In the large box at the bottom of the window, type your message. Use the arrow, **Backspace**, and **Delete** keys to review and edit the message. When you finish addressing and composing your message, click **Send Now** to send it right away.

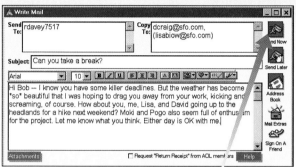

 Click

5 Close the Confirmation Dialog Box

If all is well, a dialog box will inform you that your mail has been sent. Click **OK** to close this dialog box.

Click

6 Unsending Messages

If you send a message and then have a change of heart, you *might* be able to unsend it. (The two catches are that the recipient must be an AOL member and must not have read the message yet.) Click the **Mail Center** toolbar icon and choose **Sent Mail**. (If you're already in your mailbox, just click the **Sent Mail** tab.) In the list of recently sent messages, highlight the message or messages you want to unsend and click the **Unsend** button. Click **Yes** when asked if you're sure you want to unsend the message.

Click

How-To Hints

Finding Screen Names

If you're unsure of a recipient's screen name, try finding it in AOL's Member Directory. If this doesn't work for some reason, consider telephoning your friend to get his or her screen name.

Internet Email Addresses

Internet email addresses are always in the format **user@company.name**. It's probably easiest to ask for a person's Internet email address or to have that person send you an email message so that you can read the email address in the message's **From** line. If you're an AOL member, your Internet email address is your screen name, minus any spaces, followed by **@aol.com** (for example, if your screen name is **dcraig999**, your Internet email address is **dcraig999@aol.com**). Someone who's on AOL can just email you using your screen name; someone who's not on AOL must send you email at your Internet address.

End

How to Read Usenet Newsgroups

Another built-in feature of America Online is support for Usenet newsgroups—thousands of public discussion groups that are hosted on computers around the world. When you begin using Usenet, America Online subscribes you automatically to several newsgroups. You can remove these groups and add others on topics that interest you. One of the default newsgroups on America Online is news.answers, a good place for beginners to ask questions about Usenet and the Internet.

Begin

1 Choose Newsgroups

To begin, log in to America Online. When you are connected, click the **Internet** button in the toolbar at the top of the screen and select **Newsgroups** from the drop-down menu. The **Newsgroups** window opens.

Click

2 Read Newsgroups

Click the **Read My Newsgroups** button to read newsgroups you have subscribed to. The **Read My Newsgroups** window opens.

Click

3 List Messages

You can list all the messages for a newsgroup or just the messages you have not yet read. Select the name of the newsgroup from the **My Newsgroups** list and click **List All** to see all the message subjects.

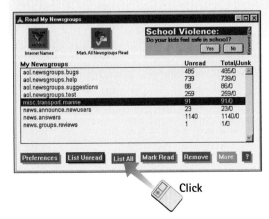

Click

4 Read a Message

From the list of subjects for the selected newsgroup, select the subject of the message you want to read and click the **Read** button.

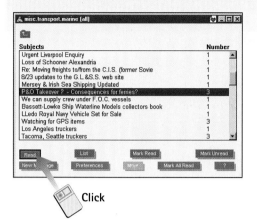

Click

5 Add a Newsgroup

If you want to subscribe to a newsgroup and you know the name of the newsgroup, click the **Expert Add** button in the **Newsgroups** window. The **Expert Add** dialog box opens.

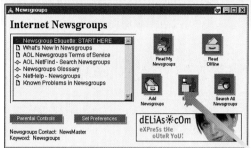

Click

6 Subscribe to the Group

Type the name of the newsgroup in the **Internet Name** text box and click the **Subscribe** button. If America Online offers the newsgroup, it will show up in the **Read My Newsgroups** window.

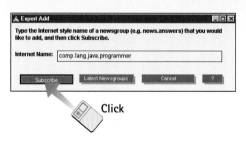

Click

End

How-To Hints

Finding Groups You Might Like

America Online has a feature that searches through the names and descriptions of Usenet newsgroups. You can use this feature to find newsgroups you might be interested in reading. To use the feature, return to the main **Newsgroups** window and click the link next to **AOL NetFind - Search Newsgroups**.

How to Use Chat Features

The **People Connection** area offers more than just the opportunity to chat in small groups in chat rooms. AOL chat helps you meet people, find out information about them (with member profiles), and even send them Instant Messages—all without leaving your chat room. Because sometimes people rub you the wrong way, you even have the option to ignore people you just don't want in your conversation. AOL's wealth of features allow you to personalize your AOL chat sessions.

Begin

1 Enter a Chat Room

Make sure that you're signed on to AOL. Click the **People** icon in the toolbar and choose **Chat Now**. A **Lobby** window opens.

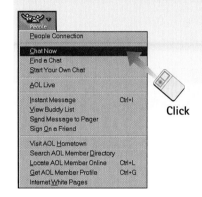

Click

2 Start Chatting

Begin participating in the chat room as you normally would.

3 Pick a Person

As you watch and participate in the chat session, one person may stand out as someone you'd like to know more about or you'd like to be able to ignore. Locate the person's screen name in the **People Here** list box and double-click that name.

Double-click

4 Get a Profile or Send a Message

A screen name window opens for the selected person. If this is a person you want to know more about, click **Get Profile** as you did in the previous task. If this is a person you'd like to send a person-to-person message to, click **Send Message**. To experiment, click **Send Message** now.

Click

5 Send an Instant Message

A **Send Instant Message** window opens with the addressee's screen name already entered in the **To** text box. Enter your message in the message box and click **Send** to begin a private person-to-person conversation. (You will learn about Instant Messages in Part 5.)

6 Ignore a Member

If you are in a room where another member's comments make you uncomfortable, select **Ignore Member** in the screen name dialog box. To return to your chat room, click the dialog box's close button. You will no longer see messages from the ignored screen name.

Click

End

How-To Hints

Handling Inappropriate Messages

If you find that a member's messages are inappropriate, click the **Notify AOL** button in the lower-right corner of the chat room window. Much like the **Notify AOL** button available in Instant Message windows, this feature allows you to notify AOL if you feel inappropriate comments are being made. Be forewarned that you'll feel the urge to do this often in some chat rooms!

More Chat Features

From any chat room window, you can gain access to a number of other chat features, including finding chat rooms of interest to you, setting up private chat sessions, setting up your chat preferences, and more. You'll learn about these features in the upcoming tasks.

How to Send Instant Messages

Instant Messages are a great way to get someone's attention—to invite him or her to join you in a chat room, ask a quick question, or just start a conversation. Each Instant Message is a private, person-to-person communication. Unlike email, Instant Messages are live interactions between two AOL members; you can only send these messages to someone who is already online. The only real delay is how long it takes to type your response and send it.

Begin

1 Open an Instant Message Window

To open an Instant Message window, click the **People** icon and choose **Instant Message**. (You can also press **Ctrl+I** to accomplish the same thing.) The **Send Instant Message** window opens.

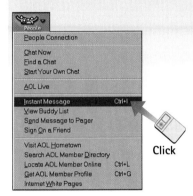

Click

2 Type the Screen Name

In the **To** box, type the screen name of the person to whom you're sending a message. To see whether your acquaintance is online before you send the message, click the **Available?** button.

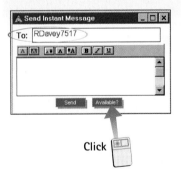

Click

3 Check Whether Person Is Online

A dialog box opens, informing you whether the person is online (you can't send Instant Messages to people who aren't online). Click **OK** to close this box.

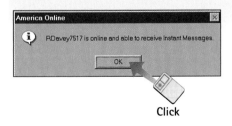

Click

4 Type and Send the Message

In the **Send Instant Message** dialog box, type your message in the text box and click **Send**.

Click

5 Respond to an Instant Message

Your acquaintance will receive the message in an **Instant Message** window that lists you as the sending party. There's a good chance he or she will write you back, in which case you'll see the message in the upper pane of an Instant Message window like this one. (You may also hear a tone to signal the incoming message.) To respond to an Instant Message, just type your response in the lower pane and click the **Send** button. If you do not want to respond to the message, click **Cancel**.

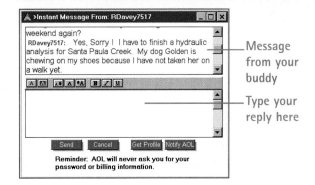

Message from your buddy

Type your reply here

6 Continue the Exchange

Continue exchanging messages with your acquaintance by entering your responses in the lower pane and clicking **Send**.

End

How-To Hints

Quick Instant Messages

If your **Buddy List** window is open (there's a good chance it will be open by default), you can send an Instant Message just by selecting the name of a buddy who's online and then clicking the **IM** button. (*IM* is online lingo for Instant Message.) Of course, this method only works for people you've designated as your buddies. Check the preceding task for details on how to do this.

Reviewing Instant Messages

If you want to review your Instant Message exchange, use the scrollbar in the upper pane of the Instant Message window.

How to Block Objectionable Content from Your AOL Account

Like many aspects of the Internet, America Online offers features you may not think are suitable for younger audiences. If you're sharing an America Online account with a child, you can set up a more restricted version of the online service by setting up parental controls. To use these controls, you must create a new screen name to which the controls will be applied. You can have up to five screen names with your America Online account.

Begin

1 Establish Controls

To begin setting up a restricted America Online screen name, click the **My AOL** button in the toolbar at the top of the screen and choose **Parental Controls**. The **AOL Parental Controls** dialog box opens.

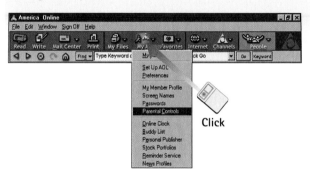

Click

2 See Screen Names

Click the **Create Screen Names** link near the bottom of the screen to open a window where you can see your current screen names, find out more about names, or create a new one. On this window, click the **Create Screen Names** link to start selecting the new name.

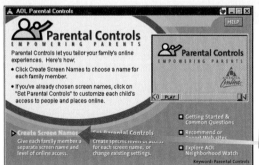

Click

3 Choose a Name

After you choose to create a new screen name, you'll have a chance to pick one for yourself. Screen names can be up to 16 characters long. Type the name you want to use and click **Continue**. In this example, the new screen name **Jax Jaguars 2000** will have parental controls applied to it.

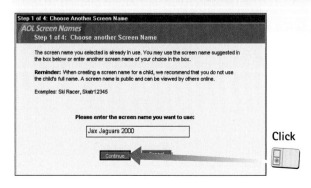

Click

4 Choose a Password

In the first text box, type the password you want to use with this screen name. In the second text box, verify the password by typing it again. The password you type for this username should be different from the one on your main America Online account. Click **Continue**.

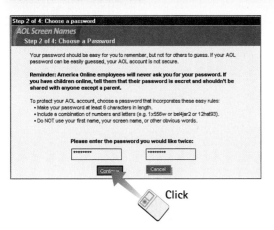

Click

5 Choose a Category

AOL offers four parental control categories; each offers a different combination of restrictions. Click the radio button next to the category you want to restrict this screen name to and click **Continue**.

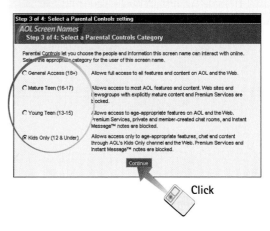

Click

6 Set Up Controls

To set up parental controls exactly as they were described in the category you picked, click the **Accept Settings** button. To make specific changes to the controls, click the **Customize Settings** button.

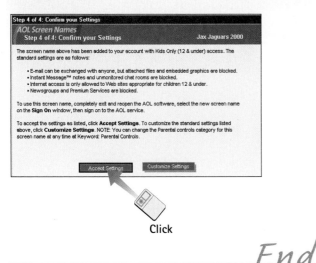

Click

How-To Hints

Testing Out a Controlled Screen Name

The best way to see whether your parental controls are suitable is to try them out. From the menu bar at the top of the screen, choose **Sign Off, Switch Screen Names**. Log in to America Online using the newly added restricted screen name and password, then try to use chat, the World Wide Web, Usenet newsgroups, and instant messaging.

End

Task

PART 10

Listening to Audio over the Internet

*O*ne of the best reasons to have high-quality speakers on your computer is the Internet. MP3 (short for MPEG-1 Audio Layer 3) is a popular format for presenting recorded sound on a computer. The format was developed with the goal of preserving sound quality while making files as small as possible.

The format has been such a success that it has moved off the computer entirely. Several companies manufacture portable MP3 players that take sound files on floppy disks instead of audio CDs.

A controversial aspect of MP3 is the lack of copy protection. MP3 files can be freely distributed after they are created. The recording industry is working to develop alternative formats that have anti-piracy protection built in.

Sound is also presented on the Internet as *streaming audio*, which begins playing immediately rather than at the end of a complete download. This format is especially well suited for live radio such as concerts.

The RealPlayer G2 and Windows Media Player are two free software programs you can install to play streaming audio files. Most media players handle multiple formats; for example, the Windows Media Player and RealPlayer both offer limited MP3 support. ●

How to Install an MP3 Player

The most popular way to present recorded music on the Internet is in MP3 format, an audio standard that stores roughly one minute of music per megabyte of disk space. To play MP3 files on your computer, you must have one of the software programs that support this format. Winamp, a free program from Nullsoft, is one of the most popular MP3 players.

Begin

1 Find the Download Page

Launch your browser, type http://www.winamp.com in the Address bar, and press **Enter**. After the Winamp Web site loads in your Web browser, click the **Get Winamp** hyperlink. A new download page opens.

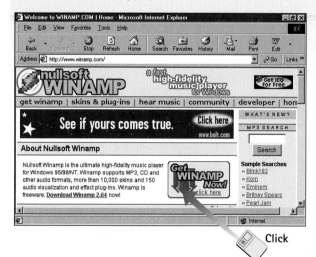

Click

2 Choose a Version

Winamp comes in basic and complete versions. Complete supports some additional sound formats (WMA and Mjuice) but takes longer to download. You may prefer to try the basic version if you are trying out MP3 for the first time. Click the appropriate radio button at the bottom of the page of the version you want to use. Click **Begin Download**.

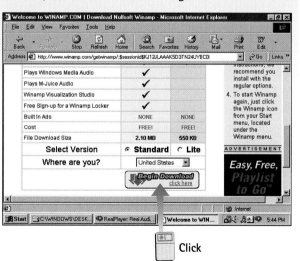

Click

3 Install from the Web

To install Winamp directly from the Web, click the radio button next to **Run this program from its current location** and then click **OK**. By running the program, you can install it immediately. When the download is complete, click the **Yes** button to run Winamp's installation program.

Click

4 Choose Winamp Settings

On the first screen after the License Agreement, you can choose which components you wish to install either by clicking check boxes or by selecting the prearranged setups in the drop-down box.

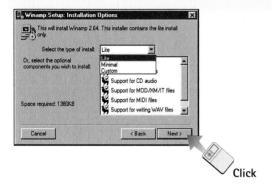

Click

5 Choose a Folder

In the second screen of the setup program, you can accept the recommended folder for Winamp or click the **Browse** button to select a different location. Click **Next** after choosing a folder.

Click

6 Identify Yourself

Continue to make your selections and click Next when appropriate. You will eventually come to the **Winamp Setup: User Information**. To stay off different mailing lists, make sure to deselect check boxes for emails you don't want.

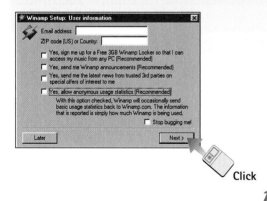

Click

End

How-To Hints

Evaluating Other MP3 Players

The World Wide Web site MP3.com has links to several MP3 players you can download. Type the URL **http://www.mp3.com** into your browser's Address bar and press **Enter** to visit this site. Look for the **Getting Started** section.

How to Find MP3 Files to Download

The MP3 format does not have copy protection, so you can download a song in MP3 format and copy it to a zip disk or to a writeable CD. For this reason, those in the recording industry don't make many songs available in MP3 format on their own Web sites or on sites for online music retailers. However, thousands of independent bands distribute their music on MP3. One of the largest archives of MP3 files is MP3.Com.

Begin

1 Visit the Site

Launch your Web browser and type `http://www.mp3.com` in the Address bar. Press **Enter**. The MP3.Com home page opens.

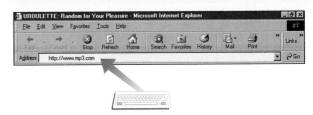

2 Browse a Genre

MP3.Com is organized into different genres, including Pop & Rock, Alternative, and Comedy. Click a hyperlink to see a list of the most-downloaded MP3 files in a category.

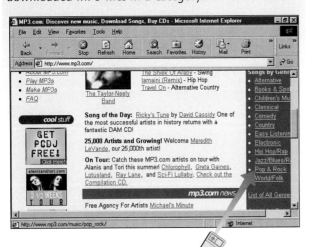

Click

3 View a Subgenre

The site is divided further into subgenres. Click a hyperlink to see groups in that category.

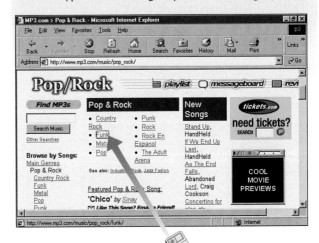

Click

4 Download a Song

When you find a song you'd like to listen to, click the **Save** hyperlink to open a dialog box that lets you choose where to store the song on your system. A dialog box with a progress bar opens to track the download of that file to your system.

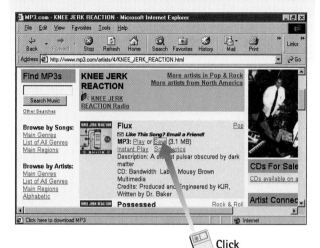

Click

5 Open a Song File

When the MP3 file has finished downloading, click the **Open** button to play it.

Click

End

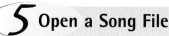

How-To Hints

Playing Samples from Recording Industry Releases

The recording industry has been slow to release material in MP3 format because of concerns over piracy, so many of the bands on MP3.Com are lesser-known professional musicians or unsigned bands. One online retailer that offers samples of commercial songs in MP3 format is CDNow. Type the URL **http://www.cdnow.com** in your Web browser's Address bar and press **Enter** to visit the site. You can search for specific groups, albums, and song titles—a musical note icon indicates songs you can sample online. Most CDNow samples are in RealAudio format, but some are offered in MP3 format.

How to Listen to an MP3 File

1 Load an MP3 File

To play an MP3 file with Winamp, open the folder that contains the file and double-click its icon. The tiny Winamp window opens and the file begins playing immediately.

There are dozens of different sound file formats, including WAV for recorded sound, RealAudio for streaming audio, and MIDI for sounds played by computer-generated instruments. MP3 has become enormously popular in a short time because it can approximate CD-quality audio in a relatively small file size and because numerous MP3 players and CD recorders are available. Several companies make portable MP3 players that can handle the same files you play with a program such as Winamp.

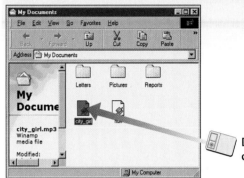

Double-click

2 Open the Equalizer

If the Winamp equalizer is not open, click the **EQ** button in the Winamp window to display it. Adjust the sliders in the Equalizer pane and click the **On** button on the Equalizer window to apply its settings to the files being played.

Click

3 Open the Playlist

Winamp also has a playlist feature that makes it possible for several MP3 files to be played in sequence. Click the **PL** button to display the playlist.

Click

4 Add to the Playlist

To add an MP3 file to the current playlist, click the **Add** button then click **Add File**. Use the Windows **File** dialog box to find the file and then click the **Open** button.

Click

5 Save a Playlist

You can save playlists to a file so that you can replay them later. Click the **List Opts** button in the Playlist window and then click **Save List**. In the **Save Playlist** dialog box that opens, give the playlist a filename and click the **Save** button.

6 Play a List

To play the songs in a stored playlist, double-click the playlist's icon.

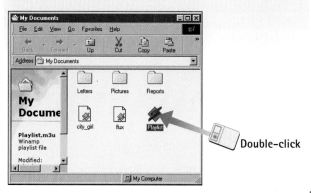

Double-click

End

How to Download a RealAudio Player

Internet Explorer 5 includes RealPlayer, multimedia software that plays back streaming RealAudio and RealVideo files. Streaming audio is played as it is downloaded, making it possible to hear the audio immediately if your Internet connection is fast enough. This format is ideal for live radio broadcasts and other presentations. The current version of RealPlayer can be downloaded for free from the developer's World Wide Web site. You also can purchase enhanced versions of the software.

Begin

1 Visit the Real Site

Launch your Web browser and visit the URL **http://www.real.com**. Click the RealPlayer **Free Download** hyperlink at the bottom of the page. The download page opens.

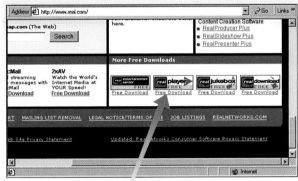

Click

2 Download RealPlayer

Real offers RealPlayer 8 Basic beta for free; the company offers an enhanced version called RealPlayer 8 Plus for sale. RealPlayer Plus G2 offers audio recording, 50 links to RealAudio channels, and other new features. To download the free version, click the **RealPlayer 8 Basic beta** hyperlink.

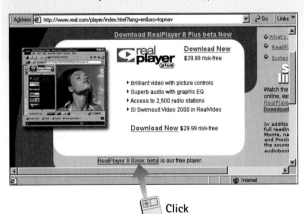

Click

3 Identify Yourself

In the form window that opens, type your name, email address, and other information. Real uses information about your computer and modem to recommend the version of RealPlayer you should download. Click the Download FREE RealPlayer 8 Basic beta button when you're done.

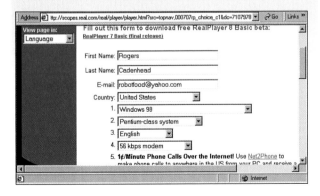

4 Choose a Version

Click a radio button associated with one of the RealPlayer versions, then click the **Download FREE RealPlayer** button.

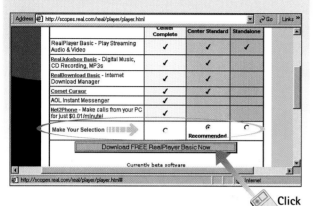

Click

5 Choose a Site

Click the hyperlink of the download site closest to your location. The **File Download** dialog box opens.

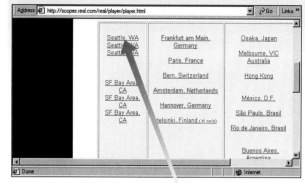

Click

6 Install Immediately

If you want to begin installing the software immediately, click the radio button next to **Run this program from its current location**, which causes the program to be installed immediately when its setup program has been downloaded to your computer. Click **OK** to begin transferring RealPlayer to your computer.

Click

End

How to Install a RealAudio Player

RealPlayer or an older version of the software can play RealAudio and RealVideo files. The preceding task described how to download the most current RealPlayer from Real, the company that developed the software. If you are running the installation program directly from the Internet, setup begins after the program has been transferred to your computer. Otherwise, open the folder where you saved the RealPlayer installation file and double-click its icon to begin setting up the software.

Begin

1 Begin Installation

In the second pane of the setup program window, review the terms and conditions of the RealPlayer software. Click **Accept** if you agree to the terms and want to install the program.

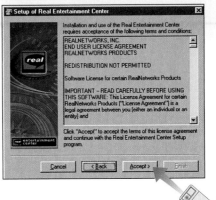

Click

2 Choose a Folder

If you want to choose a different folder to which RealPlayer should be installed, click the **Browse** button. When you have selected a folder, click **Next** to continue.

Click

3 Shortcut Time

Choose which shortcuts and items you wish to have associated with RealPlayer. Click **Finish** to continue.

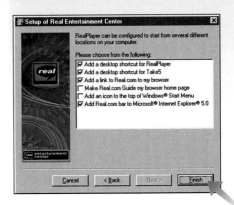

Click

4 Identify Yourself

Type your email address and zip code in the text boxes and use the drop-down list to identify your country. To stay off Real's mailing list, deselect the box next to **E-mail me about product news, updates, and offers.** Click **Next** to continue.

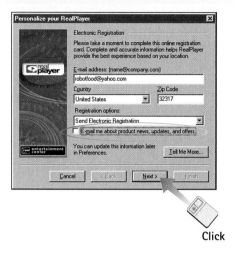

Click

5 Choose Your Speed

Use the **Connection speed** drop-down list to identify the speed of your modem, then click **Next**.

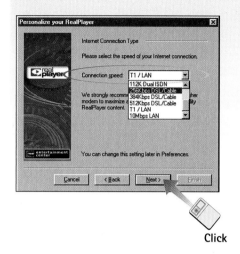

Click

6 Listen to RealAudio

RealPlayer includes preset links to dozens of radio stations broadcasting on the Internet. To tune in, open the main RealPlayer window, pull down the **Presets** menu, choose a category, and click a station's name. To stop listening to the station, click the **Stop** button on the RealPlayer window or close the RealPlayer window by choosing **File**, **Exit**.

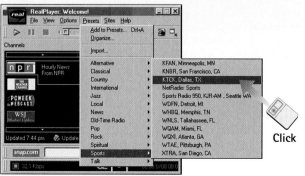

Click

How-To Hints

Listening to Radio Stations on the Internet

The RealPlayer Presets list contains only a small sampling of Internet radio stations—more than 1,000 stations around the world offer live broadcasting on the Internet. To find more stations, run your Web browser and visit **http://www.broadcast.com**.

End

How to Listen to Windows Media Player Audio Files

Microsoft has developed its own streaming multimedia software as a competitor to the RealPlayer—the Windows Media Player. You can use this free player to view video files (as described in Part 2, Task 9, "How to View Video on a Web Page"). Media Player also broadcasts streaming audio and can handle MP3 files. You can install the player along with Internet Explorer 5. For the most current version, download the program from Microsoft's Web site.

Begin

1 Find the Player

Run your Web browser and visit the **http://www.microsoft.com/windows/ mediaplayer** site. Click the **Download Windows Media Player** hyperlink.

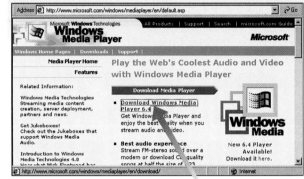

Click

2 Choose a Language

Use the drop-down list to choose the correct language version of the player. Click **Download Now** to continue. The **File Download** dialog box opens.

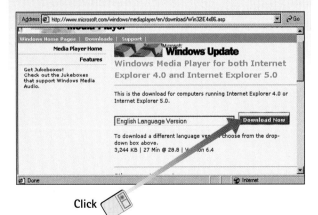

Click

3 Install from the Web

Click the radio button next to **Run this program from its current location** and click **OK**. The Windows Media Player installation program begins after its setup file has finished downloading.

Click

4 Approve Installation

A security warning is displayed before the software is installed from the Web browser. Click the **Yes** button to install Windows Media Player.

Click

5 Pick an MP3 Option

One of the formats Windows Media Player can handle is MP3. If you prefer to use Winamp or another MP3 player for sound files in that format, click the **Customize** radio button. Click **OK** to continue.

Click

6 Customize the Player

To prevent Windows Media Player from handling MP3 files, deselect the **MP3 Format Sound** box. Go through the list of file formats to see what types of media the Windows Media Player can handle. Click **Next** to continue.

Click

7 Install the Program

Choose your modem speed from the drop-down list and click **Finish** to install Windows Media Player. Visit **http://windowsmedia.microsoft.com** to obtain a guide to the multimedia files the player can present.

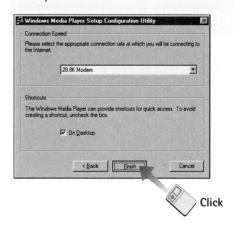

Click

End

Task

11

Shopping on the Internet

or a medium that was not allowed to be used for commerce until the current decade, the Internet has grown up quickly as a place to buy and sell. Thousands of companies now exist strictly to sell products online, including Amazon.Com and Egghead. Other companies have greatly altered their marketing strategy to offer online commerce, including Dell Computers, Barnes & Noble, and Fidelity Investments.

The Internet is also enabling new kinds of commerce to take place. The eBay auction site, which enables anyone to sell in public auctions, has been so successful at uniting buyers and sellers that some people make their living on the site. A Virginia homemaker made news by earning a six-figure salary buying wholesale and discontinued software and auctioning it through eBay and other sites such as Amazon.Com Auctions.

As a consumer, your main hesitation before purchasing online may be the security of the transaction. Online retailers offer several things to help reassure customers, including secure Web servers that keep your billing information confidential and the option to phone in your credit card number rather than send it over the Web.

How to Buy a Product over the Web

Shopping on the World Wide Web is comparable to making a purchase anywhere else: You browse through the products and services offered at a site such as CDNow or Egghead, adding items to an electronic shopping cart if you decide to purchase them. When you're ready to complete your order, you check out, removing any items from your cart that you decide not to buy after all. Amazon.Com, a trendsetter in online commerce, offers a shopping experience that's typical of these Web sites.

Begin

1 Visit a Store

To visit Amazon.Com, launch Internet Explorer 5, type the URL **http://www.amazon.com** in the Address bar, and press **Enter**. The home page for Amazon.Com opens.

2 Add an Item to Your Cart

There are thousands of pages on Amazon.Com describing products for sale. When you find something you want to purchase, click the **Add to Shopping Cart** button.

Click

3 Review Your Cart

Amazon.Com displays the contents of your shopping cart when you add an item. To purchase multiple copies of the same item, type a different number in the **Qty** text box.

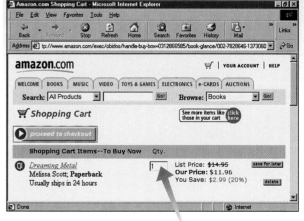

4 Remove an Item

To remove an item from your shopping cart, click the **delete** button associated with that item.

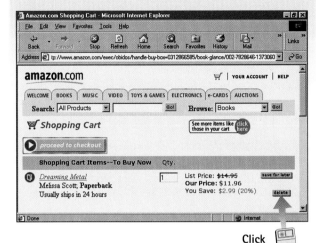

Click

5 Proceed to Checkout

When you're ready to purchase the items in your cart, you can begin the process of buying them by clicking the **proceed to checkout** button. The process of purchasing an item is covered in the next task, "How to Shop Safely on the Web."

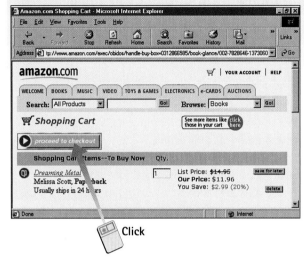

Click

End

How-To Hints

Finding Stores on the World Wide Web

Each of the major portal sites offers directories of online stores; some sites such as Yahoo! sell products themselves. A quick way to find the largest list of Internet retailers is to visit the SHOPsheet Web site. Type the URL **http://www.shopsheet.com** into your browser's Address bar and press **Enter**.

How to Shop Safely on the Web

Most purchases on the World Wide Web are made with a credit or debit card. When you decide to buy a product, you enter your mailing and purchase information using a Web page. The store bills your card and ships the product, often sending an email message to notify you when the product has been shipped. This process should always take place on a *secure Web server* to protect the confidentiality of your billing information.

Begin

1 Use a Secure Server

When you're ready to purchase something at an online store such as Amazon.Com, a hyperlink is presented to the store's secure Web server. Click this link to load a confidential ordering page.

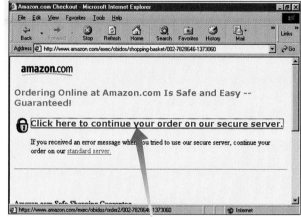

 Click

2 Check the Server

When Internet Explorer 5 loads a page from a secure server, a padlock icon is displayed along the browser's lower edge. If you don't see this icon, it's inadvisable to provide confidential information such as your credit card number on the site.

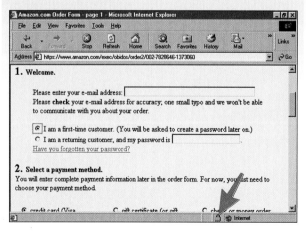

3 Identify Yourself

Type your email address in the appropriate text box. If you have never shopped at Amazon.Com before, click the **I am a first-time customer** radio button.

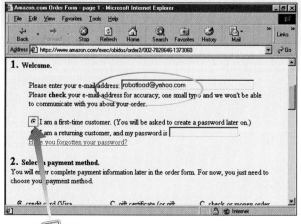

Click

4 Select a Payment Method

Click the radio button associated with the payment method you want to use and then click the **continue** button. You'll be asked to choose a shipping method and to provide your mailing address.

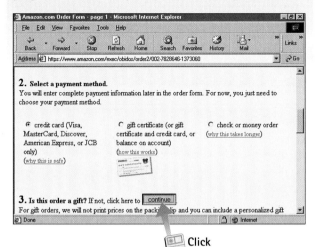

Click

5 Provide Ordering Info

If you are ordering by credit card, you'll be asked for your billing information. Amazon.Com offers the option of omitting your full credit card number and calling an 800 number to provide it.

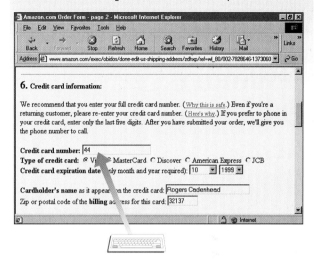

6 Choose a Password

If you're a first-time customer, type a password you'll use to identify yourself when making future orders and click the **continue** button.

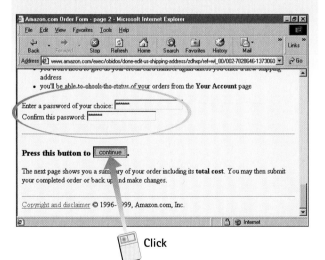

Click

7 Confirm Your Order

Amazon.Com presents the cost of your order and where it will be shipped. If everything looks correct, and you want to make the purchase, click the **Click Here to Send Us Your Order** button.

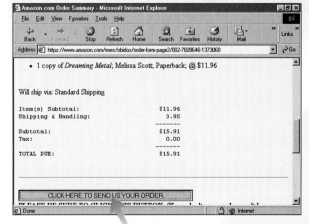

Click

End

How to Participate in Online Auctions

When the eBay World Wide Web site was launched, a new form of Internet shopping took hold—the world's largest garage sale. eBay acts as a middle-man in online auctions, charging a small fee or a percentage from people who sell products through the site. Anyone is free to buy or sell items, using a unique bidding system that keeps your maximum bid secret until after a sale. Users vouch for each other and report fraudulent transactions by contributing feedback ratings that are published about each user.

Begin

1 Visit eBay

Launch your Web browser, type the URL **http://www.ebay.com** in the Address bar, and press **Enter**. The eBay home page opens.

2 Create an Account

Before you can buy or sell anything, you must register so that eBay can confirm that you're using a valid email address. Click the **Register** hyperlink.

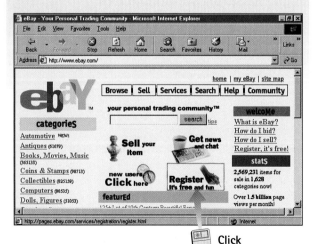

Click

3 Use a Secure Server

Select your country from the list box. If you want to sign up using eBay's secure Web server, check the **register using SSL** box. To continue, click **Begin the registration process now**.

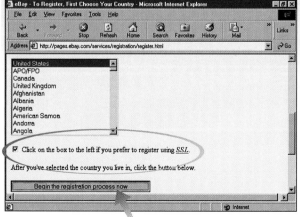

Click

4 Identify Yourself

Fill out the registration form with your name, email address, mailing address, and any optional information you choose to provide. When you're done, click the **continue** button.

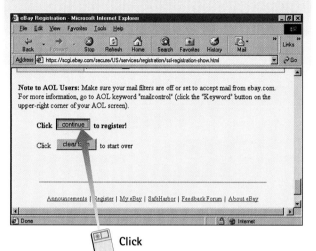

Click

5 Finish the Registration

Click the **submit** button to send your new registration to eBay. A confirmation code will be emailed to the address you used during registration.

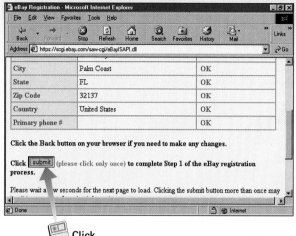

Click

6 Confirm Registration

The confirmation letter from eBay should arrive within 24 hours. When it does, make a note of your confirmation code and click the hyperlink included in the letter.

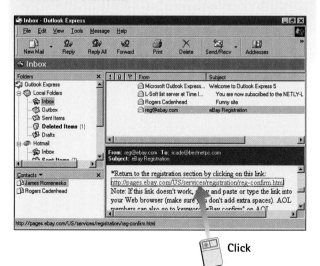

Click

7 Set Up an Account

When you return to the eBay site with your confirmation code, you'll be asked for your email address and the code. You'll also be able to pick your own username and password. To finish, click **Complete your registration**.

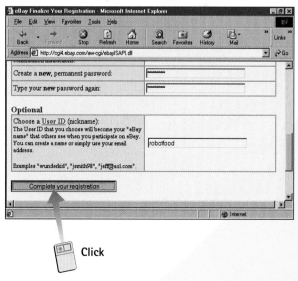

Click

End

How to Bid in an Online Auction

The preceding task covered how to register for a free account with the online auction site eBay. After you have an account, you can make bids in current auctions and sign up to sell items of your own. Bidding in auctions is free; you'll be notified by email if someone else outbids you. You also will receive email if you win an auction. When you win, you must contact the seller within 72 hours to arrange payment.

Begin

1 Search for Auctions

Launch your Web browser, type the URL `http://www.ebay.com` in the Address bar, and press **Enter**. To look for a certain item in current auctions, type the name of the item or a description of the item in the search box and click the **search** button.

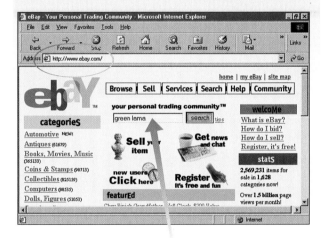

2 List Auctions

Any current auctions matching your search criteria are listed, along with the recent high bids. To find out more about an auction, click its hyperlink.

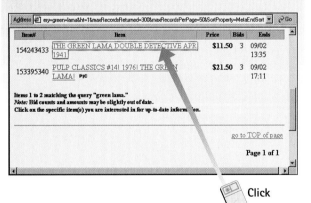

Click

3 View User Feedback

Every eBay user has a *feedback rating*—a numeric ranking listed with his or her username. To view feedback that has been submitted about a seller, click the number next to the seller's username. You'll see a page listing comments that have been made by eBay users who have dealt with this person in the past.

Click

4 Make a Bid

To make a bid in an auction, type your maximum bid in the text box and click the **review bid** button.

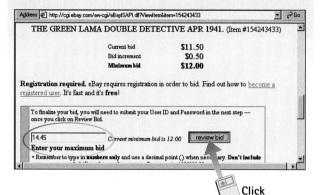

Click

5 Confirm Your Bid

When you bid on eBay, your *maximum* bid is kept secret until after the auction. Your *actual* bid is the minimum amount needed to raise the current high bid. Click **place bid** to confirm your bid.

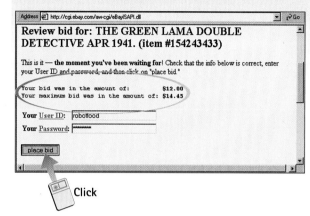

Click

6 Bid Again

If your maximum bid turns out to be lower than someone else's bid, that user's bid will increase to outbid you. If you want to submit a higher bid, click the **bid again** hyperlink.

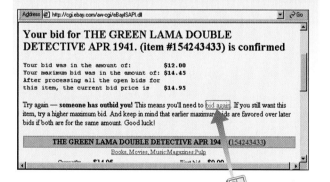

Click

7 Bookmark an Auction

If you become the high bidder in an auction, you'll be sent an email if another user outbids you. To bookmark an auction page to make it easy to return to that page, make sure that the page is open in the browser, pull down the **Favorites** menu, and choose **Add to Favorites**.

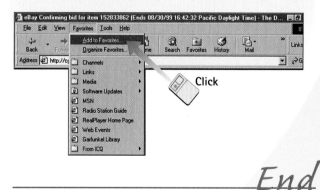

Click

End

Task

PART 12

Investigating Stocks, Taxes, and Savings on the Web

The Internet is changing the way many industries function, but one of the most drastic alterations has taken place in stock investing. Before the popularization of the World Wide Web, most investors bought and sold stocks by communicating with a professional broker in person or by telephone. Because this kind of service is expensive for a brokerage to provide, transaction fees for a single purchase were routinely $50 or more.

Although you can still deal personally with a broker, millions of investors are buying and selling stocks directly over the Web. They use online brokerages such as Datek and E*TRADE, placing and fulfilling an order quickly without the assistance of a professional broker. Transaction fees have dropped as low as $7.95.

The World Wide Web also brings information to investors that was not readily available to the public, such as technical analysis, historical data that can be immediately plugged into spreadsheets, and business news wires.

In addition to dozens of professional stock sites, you can use the Web for advice and information about other aspects of your financial well-being. These areas include taxes, savings, and mutual fund investments. ●

How to Find Current Stock Quotes

Dozens of World Wide Web sites cater to stock market investors, including popular portals such as Yahoo!, Lycos, and the Microsoft Network. Several excellent sites offer free 15-minute–delayed stock quotes, historical stock price information, discussion forums, and investment information. To get stock quotes without the 15-minute delay, you can join one of the online brokerages that help you trade stocks online.

Begin

1 Visit a Stock Site

One free site that specializes in technical stock analysis is ClearStation. To visit this site, launch your Web browser, type the URL **http://www.clearstation.com** in the Address bar, and press **Enter**. The ClearStation home page loads.

2 Look Up a Quote

Current stock quotes can be viewed by using the stock's *ticker symbol*—a short, unique code assigned to the company by the exchange it trades on. Type the ticker symbol in the **Enter Symbol** text box and click the **Get Graphs!** hyperlink. The most recent price and a historical price graph will be displayed on a new page.

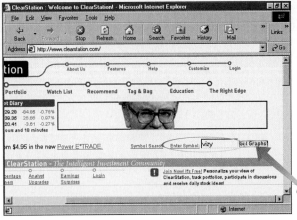

Click

3 Read News

To see recent news stories and press releases that mention the stock you're investigating, click the **News Articles** hyperlink. Any available information is presented on a new Web page.

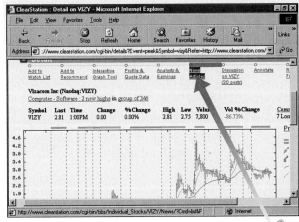

Click

4 Find a Symbol

If you don't know a company's ticker symbol, click the **Symbol Search** hyperlink. A search page is displayed.

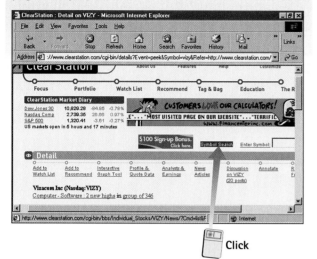

Click

5 Search for a Company

To begin a search, type the name of the company you're looking for in the search box and then click the **Submit Query** button.

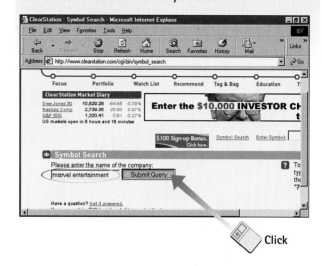

Click

6 View Search Results

All companies that match the search name are listed. Click a ticker symbol to view the current stock price and other information about that stock.

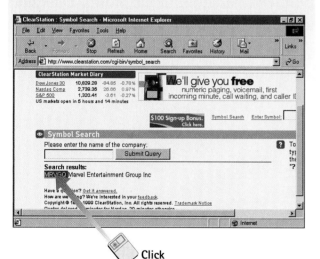

Click

End

How-To Hints

Finding Other Stock-Tracking Web Sites

ClearStation is a great resource for investors who make use of technical indicators such as the MACD and stochastic graphs. Depending on your investment strategy, you may find the services offered by other stock information sites to be more useful. Visit the following URLs to try out other stock market sites:

- ✓ **Yahoo! Finance:**
  http://quote.yahoo.com

- ✓ **The Motley Fool:**
  http://www.fool.com

- ✓ **Lycos Investing:**
  http://investing.lycos.com

- ✓ **Microsoft MoneyCentral:**
  http://moneycentral.msn.com

How to Create a Portfolio of Stocks You Track

Many World Wide Web sites that offer stock information can store a list of the stocks you're interested in—either because you own them or are thinking about buying them. If you own a stock, you can enter its purchase price and number of shares, and the site will display the current worth of your portfolio. To make use of these timesaving services, you must *join* a site to acquire your own username and password.

Begin

1 Join a Site

To join ClearStation, visit **http://www.clearstation.com**. When the home page loads, click the **Join Now** hyperlink.

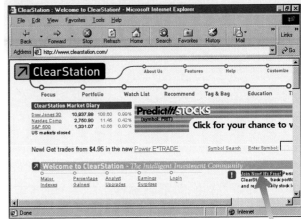

Click

2 Identify Yourself

Fill out the text boxes on the ClearStation membership form and then click the **Join** button.

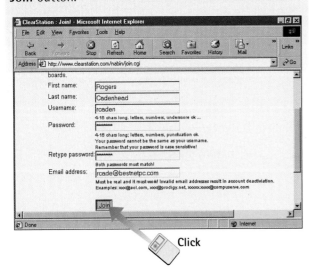

Click

3 Set Up Your Portfolio

To start your portfolio with a list of the stocks you currently own, type their ticker symbols in the **Portfolio Stocks** text box. Type a space (no commas) between symbols. Also type a name for this portfolio in the **Portfolio Name** text box. Click the **Start Portfolio Build** button to continue.

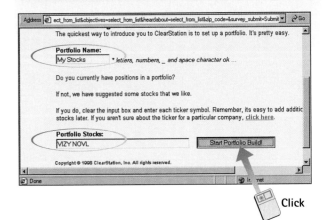

Click

4 Describe Your Stocks

To complete your portfolio, provide price and quantity information about the stocks you have purchased. Click **Finish Portfolio Build** when you're done. The **Watch List Configuration** page opens.

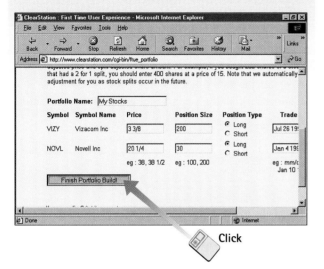

Click

5 Set Up a Watch List

You can use ClearStation to monitor stocks you don't yet own by adding them to a watch list. To start your list, type ticker symbols in the **Watch List stocks** text box and click **Build Watch List**.

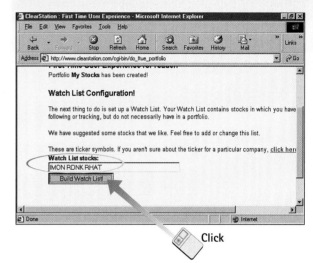

Click

6 Create the Watch List

Click the **Finish Watch List Build** button to add the watch list to your portfolio and to create the portfolio.

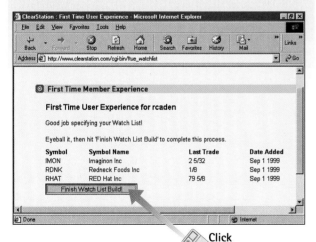

Click

How-To Hints

Entering the Purchase Price of a Stock

When you're adding a stock to a portfolio on ClearStation, you can use the fractional form of the stock price—such as 20 1/4 or 5 1/2. Many portfolio-tracking Web sites support this feature because stock prices are traditionally presented using fractions rather than decimals. Otherwise, make a note of the price as a decimal when you purchase a stock so that you can enter this price into a portfolio-management Web site.

End

TASK 3

How to Add and Remove Stocks from a Portfolio

Sites such as ClearStation and The Motley Fool offer a chance to manage a portfolio you've established with a brokerage. After buying or selling a stock through your brokerage, you make note of the purchase details on your portfolio management Web site. On ClearStation, in addition to your actual portfolio (which is private), you can create a public portfolio of stocks that you recommend. ClearStation users can subscribe to the public portfolios of other people and will receive email whenever a change is made.

Begin

1 View Your Portfolios

Visit ClearStation at the URL **http://www.clearstation.com**. When the home page opens, click the **Portfolio** hyperlink. A new page opens, listing your portfolios and recommended list.

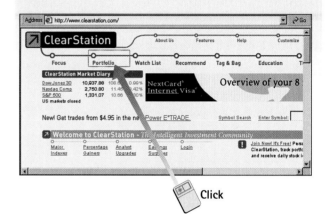

Click

2 Choose a Portfolio

All your portfolios are displayed with their stocks' performances today and their current values. To view a portfolio in more detail, click its name.

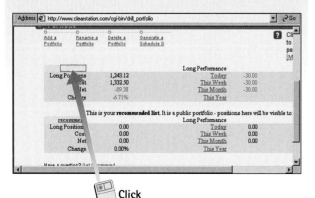

Click

3 See a Stock

Click the ticker symbol of a stock to view more information about that stock.

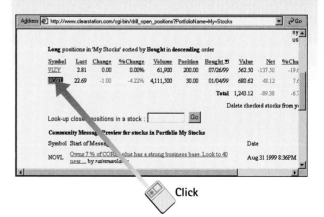

Click

172 PART 12: INVESTIGATING TAXES, STOCKS, AND SAVINGS ON THE WEB

4 Delete a Stock

To remove a stock from your portfolio, first display the details of that stock (see Step 3). In the **Actions** column, click the **Delete** hyperlink. A confirmation page will be displayed. Click the **Delete** button to remove the stock from your portfolio and add it to your watch list.

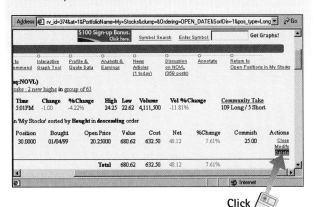

Click

5 Add a Stock

To add a stock to your portfolio, first display your portfolio in ClearStation. Then click the **Enter New Positions** hyperlink. The page adjusts to provide an area in which you can type additions to the portfolio.

Click

6 Enter the Symbol

Type one or more ticker symbols in the **Stocks** text box, separating the symbols with spaces, then click the **Add** button.

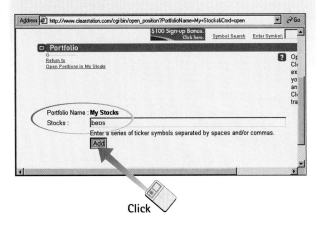

Click

7 Describe Your Purchase

Enter the purchase price, the number of shares bought, and other details of the transaction you conducted when you bought the stock through a brokerage. Click the **Add these stocks to your Portfolio** button.

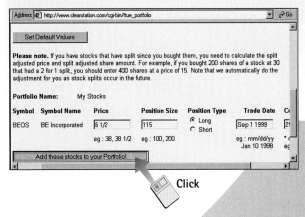

Click

End

How to Get Tax Help Online

When tax time comes around each April in the United States, one of the places you can go for help is the World Wide Web. In addition to the federal government's extensive Internal Revenue Service site, you can get information on taxes you owe—and how to reduce them—from places such as Microsoft MoneyCentral, Money.Com, and Yahoo! Finance.

Begin

1 Visit Money Central

Launch your Web browser, type the URL **http://www.moneycentral.com** in the Address bar, and press **Enter**. The MoneyCentral home page opens.

2 View Tax Information

MoneyCentral is divided into sections on savings, retirement, insurance, taxes, and other financial topics. Click the **Taxes** hyperlink to go to the taxes page.

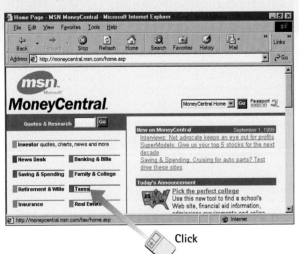

Click

3 Estimate Your Taxes

To get an estimate of what you owe on your current taxes, click the **Estimate your taxes** hyperlink. The **Tax Estimator** window opens.

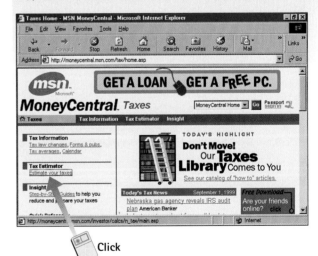

Click

4 Get Help with an Item

The MoneyCentral Tax Estimator requires you to fill out several forms. Fill out the forms as they are presented. If you are unsure about an item, click the mouse in that item's text box to see a description of the field in the text area to the right of the form, under the **Help** graphic.

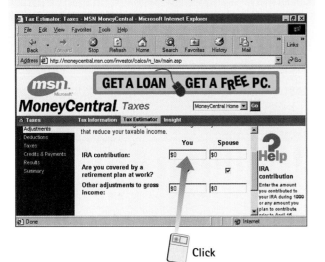

 Click

5 Download Tax Forms

The Internal Revenue Service offers tax forms you can download from the Web and print out. To find these forms, click the **Forms & pubs** hyperlink in the navigation bar on the left side of the screen. An informational screen opens.

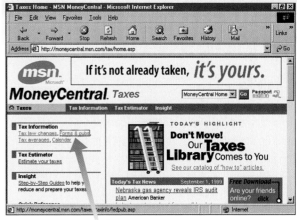

 Click

6 Visit the IRS Site

Click the **retrieve forms and instructions** hyperlink to visit the forms section of the Internal Revenue Service site. You can select the forms you want to download from that site.

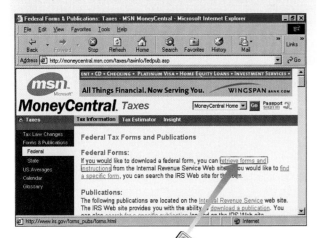

Click

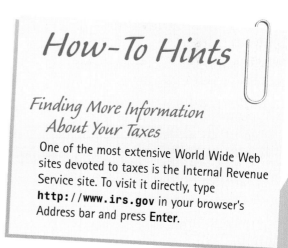

How-To Hints

Finding More Information About Your Taxes

One of the most extensive World Wide Web sites devoted to taxes is the Internal Revenue Service site. To visit it directly, type **http://www.irs.gov** in your browser's Address bar and press **Enter**.

End

How to Find Savings Tips Online

The World Wide Web has thousands of sites enticing you to spend money. On many of the financial sites mentioned in the tasks in this part, you can find tips and tools for moving money in the opposite direction—to your savings. One good example of a savings tool is the investment earnings calculator offered by Money.Com, a service of *Money Magazine*. That site also offers a searchable database of mutual funds.

Begin

1 Load the Financial Site

To visit Money.Com, launch your Web browser, type the URL **http://www.money.com** in the Address bar, and press **Enter**. The Money.Com home page opens.

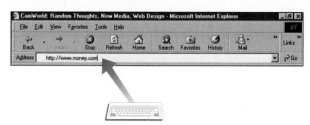

2 Use a Savings Calculator

Click the **Retirement** hyperlink to find the site's savings calculator. Fill in values for **Initial deposit**, **Interest rate**, and the other text boxes. Click **Calculate** to display the final value of your nest egg on a new Web page.

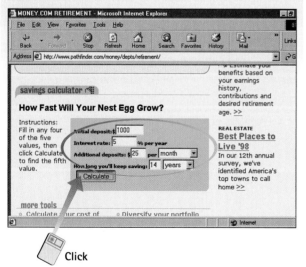

Click

3 Research Mutual Funds

In the **More Tools** section of the page, click the **Find the right mutual fund** hyperlink to search Money.Com's database of mutual funds and to find one that meets your investment goals and matches the amount of risk you're willing to take.

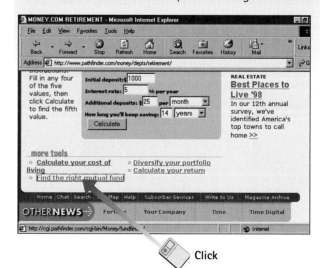

Click

4 Search the Database

You can set different criteria for mutual funds you're investigating, including the amount of risk you want to take, the kind of fees that are charged, and the rate of return. Click the **Show results** hyperlink to see a list of funds that match the criteria you've entered.

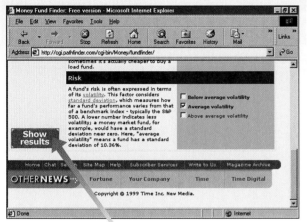

Click

5 View a Fund

To find out more about a fund that meets your search criteria, click the ticker symbol hyperlink next to the fund's name. A new page opens, displaying information about that particular fund.

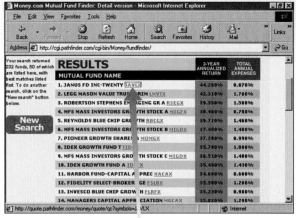

Click

End

How-To Hints

Staying on Top of Financial and Investment News

Several World Wide Web sites specialize in financial news and analyses written by expert commentators and journalists. To visit these sites, type the following URLs in your browser's Address bar and press **Enter**:

✓ **TheStreet.Com:** http://www.thestreet.com

✓ **Briefing.Com:** http://www.briefing.com

✓ **CBS MarketWatch:** http://cbs.marketwatch.com

Task

Creating Your Own Web Site

*A*nyone can publish on the World Wide Web. As you become acquainted with this medium, the benefits and the drawbacks of this editorial freedom should become apparent quickly. The Web is the most chaotic and grassroots medium that has ever been devised: It gives individual, low-budget publishers an unprecedented opportunity to build a worldwide audience.

No better proof of this exists than the career of Internet gossip Matt Drudge. Working alone out of a Los Angeles apartment, Drudge decided to act as a modern-day Walter Winchell, reporting rumors and describing upcoming media stories in advance of their publication at the URL **http://www.drudgereport.com**. When he advanced a *Newsweek* magazine story about President Clinton and Monica Lewinsky in early 1998, Drudge attracted more visitors to his one-man site than many of the large media outlets with staffs numbering in the hundreds.

With software included with your operating system, you can create Web pages, link them together, and test them in your own Web browser. When you're done, you can publish your own site and compete for attention with every other page on the Web. ●

How to Install Web Publishing Software

One of the optional programs you can install with Windows 98 is FrontPage Express, a pared-down version of Microsoft's World Wide Web publishing software. FrontPage Express enables you to create and format a Web page as easily as you author documents in a word processor. If you are comfortable using Microsoft Word, you should be able to master FrontPage Express quickly. And you don't even have to learn HTML (the text markup language used to create Web pages).

Begin

1 Open the Control Panel

To install FrontPage Express, place your Windows 98 installation CD in the CD-ROM drive. Click the **Start** button, open the **Settings** folder, and click **Control Panel**. The **Control Panel** window opens.

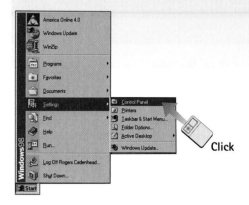
Click

2 Add a Program

Click the **Add/Remove Programs** icon. The **Add/Remove Programs Properties** dialog box opens.

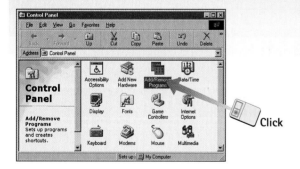
Click

3 Change Your Windows Setup

Click the **Windows Setup** tab to see a list of the programs that were installed along with Windows. To see the Internet programs on your computer, select the **Internet Tools** item and then click the **Details** button. The **Internet Tools** dialog box opens.

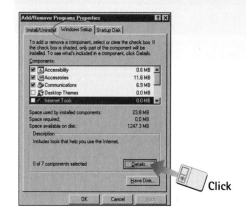
Click

4 Choose FrontPage Express

Check the box next to **Microsoft FrontPage Express** to select this program for installation, then click the **OK** button. The **Internet Tools** dialog box closes.

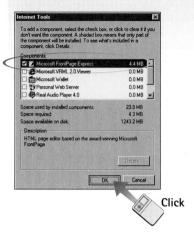

Click

5 Install the Program

Back in the **Add/Remove Programs Properties** dialog box, click the **OK** button to begin the installation of FrontPage Express. A **Copying Files** dialog box appears as files are copied from the Windows 98 CD to your computer. When the installation is complete, the **Add/Remove Program Properties** dialog box automatically closes.

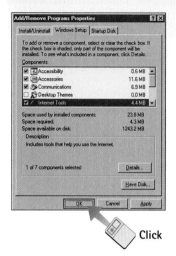

Click

6 Run FrontPage Express

When the setup process is complete, you can use the newly installed program. To run the program, click the **Start** button, choose **Programs**, choose **Internet Explorer**, and then click **FrontPage Express**. The following task explains how to use the software you've just installed.

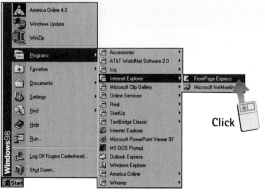

Click

How-To Hints

Finding Other Versions of FrontPage

FrontPage Express is a greatly simplified version of Microsoft's FrontPage Web-development software. FrontPage 2000, the current version, is part of the Office 2000 suite of programs. You also can buy it separately. To find out more about the commercial versions of FrontPage, type
http://www.microsoft.com/frontpage in your browser's Address bar and press **Enter**.

End

How to Add Text and Color to a Web Page

If you have ever used a word processor, you've developed most of the skills you need to create Web pages using software such as FrontPage Express. Web pages are simple text documents with hidden formatting tags that control how a Web browser such as Internet Explorer 5 or Netscape Navigator displays the document. FrontPage Express handles most of this formatting for you so that you can focus on the content of your documents.

Begin

1 Run FrontPage Express

To launch the FrontPage Express program, click the **Start** button, and choose **Programs, Internet Explorer, FrontPage Express**. FrontPage Express opens a new blank Web page for you to work on.

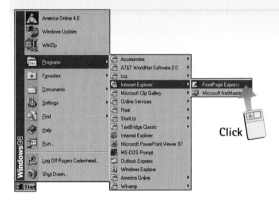

Click

2 Add Text to a Page

To add text to the blank page FrontPage presents you with, just start typing in the main editing area.

3 Create a Heading

By default, the text you type on a Web page starts out as body text (called Normal style). You can change some of this text into a *heading*. To turn text into a heading, first select the text by clicking and dragging your mouse over it. Then choose a heading from the **Formatting** drop-down list in the toolbar at the top of the page. Headings range in size from **Heading1** (large) to **Heading6** (small).

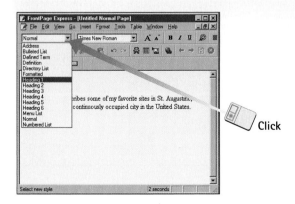

Click

4 Choose Colors

One way to enliven a Web page is to pick different colors for the page background, text, and hyperlinks. Start by selecting a background color: Pull down the **Format** menu and click **Background**. The **Page Properties** dialog box opens.

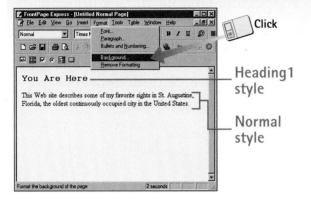

Click

— Heading1 style

— Normal style

5 Pick a Background

To change the background color, click the **Background** tab to bring it to the front. Click the arrow next to the **Background** list item and then choose the desired color from the drop-down list that appears. Click **OK** to apply the change to the Web page you're working on.

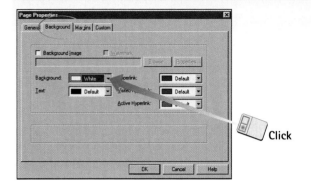

Click

6 Save the Page

When you're ready to save the Web page, select **File, Save As**. The **Save As** dialog box opens.

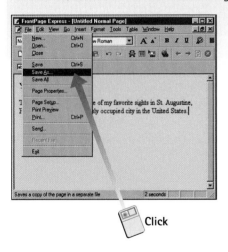

Click

7 Save to Disk

Click the **As File** button. A dialog box opens that enables you to pick a folder and a filename for your Web page file. If the page you're saving is the main page of a site (or if it's the only page), give it the filename **index.html** (this name indicates that this page is the home page of a Web site). Click **OK** twice to close both dialog boxes and save the page with the filename you specified to a folder on your computer.

Click

End

How to Add a Link to a Web Page

The most important difference between World Wide Web pages and most other documents is hyperlinks. A *hyperlink* connects a Web page to any other file that's accessible on the Web, whether it's stored on the same server or on a Web server on the other side of the planet. Clicking a hyperlink opens the related document, which can be a page, a graphics file, or any other type of file. You can associate a hyperlink with any part of a Web page: text, images, programs, or a combination of all three.

Begin

1 Open a Web Page

To open a Web page in FrontPage Express, choose **File, Open**. In the **Open** dialog box, click the **Browse** button to choose the Web page on your computer that you want to open.

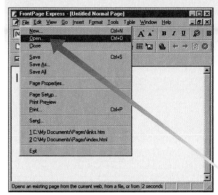

Click

2 Add a Hyperlink

To add a hyperlink to text, click and drag your mouse over the text you want to select. With this text highlighted, choose **Insert, Hyperlink**. The **Create Hyperlink** dialog box opens.

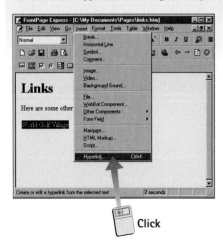

Click

3 Choose the Linked URL

Click the **World Wide Web** tab to bring it to the front. In the **URL** box, type the URL of the file you want to appear when a user clicks the hyperlink you're creating. Then click the **OK** button. The same technique works for images and other page elements you want to associate with a hyperlink: Highlight the thing on a page that should have a link and choose **Insert, Hyperlink**.

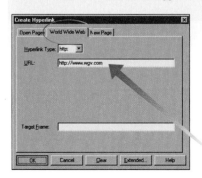

4 Link to a Page

Hyperlinks don't have to use a full URL—an address you enter in a browser to load a document. Instead, when you are linking to a file in the same folder, you can use a partial URL that contains only the name of the file. Start by selecting the text you want to make into a hyperlink and then open the **Create Hyperlink** dialog box (choose **Insert, Hyperlink**).

Click

5 Choose the Page

On the World Wide Web tab, in the **URL** text box, type the name of the file you want the hyperlink to reference and click the **OK** button. Although most hyperlinks you create will be to Web pages—which have **.HTML** or **.HTM** extensions—you can link to any kind of file.

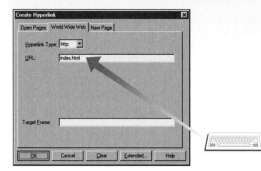

6 Save the Page

To save the Web page you're currently editing in FrontPage Express, choose **File, Save**. If the file has not been saved before, you are given the opportunity to name the file and select the directory or folder in which to store the file.

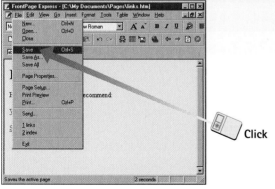

Click

How-To Hints

Creating Quick Hyperlinks to Pages in FrontPage Express

A fast way to create hyperlinks to your own Web pages is to first open all the pages in FrontPage Express. When all pages are open for editing, select text to associate a hyperlink with and choose **Insert, Hyperlink**. Click the **Open Pages** tab in the **Create Hyperlink** dialog box. You'll see a list of pages that are open in FrontPage Express. Select a page and click **OK** to quickly create a hyperlink to that page.

End

How to Add a Graphic to a Web Page

You include graphics in your Web pages by inserting image files on the page. Most Web browsers can display graphics in the GIF and JPG formats; some include support for alternative formats such as PNG. Before you insert images into a Web page you're creating in FrontPage Express, move the image files to the same folder that contains the Web page. Note that image files are not combined with or inserted into a Web page when you include them on a page; they are *published* to the Web server along with the pages that display them.

Begin

1 Choose a Location

In the editing area of the FrontPage Express page you are working with, click the mouse at the place you want to insert the image file.

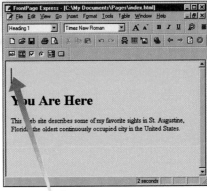

Click

2 Insert the Image

Choose **Insert, Image** to open the **Image** dialog box.

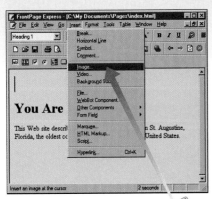

Click

3 Find the File

On the **Other Location** tab, click the **Browse** button to open another dialog box from which you can select the graphics file you want to display.

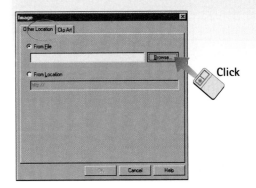
Click

4 Open the File

Browse to the image file you want to insert on your Web page and select the file. Click the **Open** button to choose a file, then click the **OK** button on the Image dialog box to insert the file on the Web page.

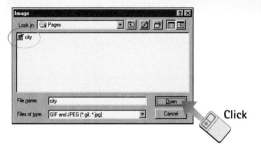

Click

5 Add a Hyperlink to the Graphic

To associate a hyperlink with an image, click the image to select it and then choose **Insert, Hyperlink**. The familiar **Create Hyperlink** dialog box opens, which you can use to locate and select the file you want to associate with the graphic.

Click

End

How-To Hints

Linking to an Email Address

You also can create a *mailto* hyperlink—a special kind of link to an email address instead of to a Web document. When a mailto link is clicked in a Web browser configured to work with an email program, the email program starts a new message. The recipient of this new message is the email address in the mailto link. To create a mailto hyperlink, begin with the text **mailto:** followed by the email address. For example, **mailto:president@whitehouse.gov** is a mailto hyperlink to the official email address of the U.S. president. Mailto hyperlinks can appear anywhere other links appear.

How to Test a Web Site You Created

Before you make your Web pages available on the World Wide Web, you should test them completely on your own computer. If you set up your hyperlinks and graphics correctly on your local system, you should be able to view each of the pages you created without being connected to the Internet. These pages should be connected to each other with hyperlinks so that a visitor can see all related pages in your site. If you *are* connected to the Internet, you also can test all the hyperlinks on your Web pages that refer to other Web sites.

Begin

1 Open the Home Page

A group of related Web pages is called a *Web site*; the main page of a site is called its *home page*. To view your site's home page, open the folder containing the pages you created and double-click the **index** or **index.html** icon—**index** is the standard name for a site's home page. Your primary Web browser launches and loads that Web page.

 Double-click

2 Test a Hyperlink

Text hyperlinks you created are formatted, by default, in a different color and are underlined. Click a hyperlink to test whether it works. If the page you are expecting to load actually loads in your Web browser window, the hyperlink works.

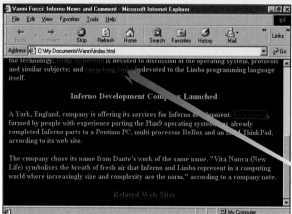

Click

3 Return to the Site

If you are connected to the Internet, you can check the hyperlinks that leave your Web pages (that is, the links to pages other than those on your local computer). After your browser has loaded the page the hyperlink directed it to, click the **Back** button to return to the page you were on when you clicked the hyperlink (in this case, your site's home page).

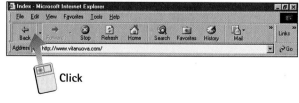

Click

4 Check All Local Links

When you are testing your site, you should check all the hyperlinks that connect to pages on your site. You should be able to reach each page you have created. Click a hyperlink to try it out.

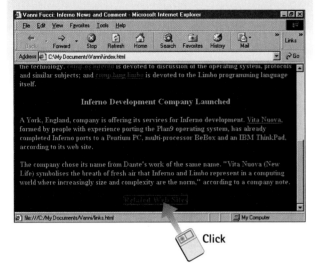

Click

5 Close the Browser

When you're done testing, or you have to fix a page or a hyperlink in FrontPage Express, close your browser by choosing **File, Close**. Then launch FrontPage Express, open the page you want to correct, and make the necessary changes. Save the page when you are done.

Click

End

How-To Hints

Fixing Broken Hyperlinks with FrontPage Express

To fix a broken hyperlink in FrontPage Express, select the text or image being hyperlinked and choose **Insert, Hyperlink**. The current hyperlink appears in the dialog box that opens. You can type a new hyperlink in the **URL** box or click the **Clear** button to delete the hyperlink entirely. (Note that deleting the hyperlink does not affect the text or image on the page to which the hyperlink was added.)

Testing Web Pages with Different Browsers

More than 33 percent of all World Wide Web users use Netscape Navigator to visit pages. If you are publishing pages on the World Wide Web, make sure that you test those pages with both Internet Explorer and Netscape Navigator. You learn how to install a second browser in Part 14, "Using Netscape Navigator to Browse the Web."

How to Join a Free Web Provider to Host Your Site

Some Internet service providers offer free Web hosting as part of your subscription. They provide from 1 to 10 megabytes of disk space for the files you want to make available on your site. These files must be *published* (transferred from your computer to your provider's Web server). Dozens of companies offer free Web hosting, including Yahoo!, Tripod, and HomePage.Com. These services require only that you have a valid email address to join.

Begin

1 Join a Free Service

One of the easiest free Web hosts to join is HomePage.Com. To load the home page for this site, launch your Web browser, type the URL **http://www.homepage.com** in the Address bar, and press **Enter**.

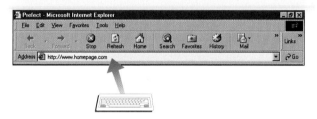

2 Choose a Name

Type a short name that describes your site in the **Name** text box and click the **Reserve it!** button. If the name isn't available, you'll see a message alerting you to that fact. Click your browser's **Back** button to return to this page and type a different name. The name you pick will be used as part of the site's Web address (URL).

3 Sign Up for a Site

If the name you want to give your Web site is available, you can sign up immediately. Type your email address in the text box and click the **Reserve it!** button.

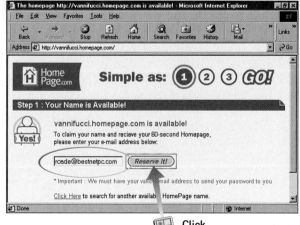

 Click

4 Identify Yourself

To request your free HomePage.Com Web site, fill out the form that appears. You'll have to describe yourself and the site you will be publishing. Read through the terms and conditions of the service; if you agree to them, click the **Agree & Continue** button.

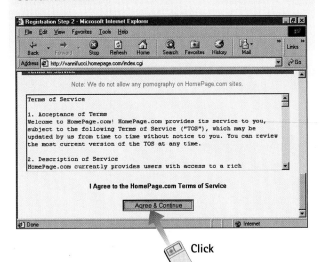

Click

5 Visit Your Site

HomePage.Com puts a temporary Web site up until you can publish your own Web pages. Click the site's hyperlink to see what's currently online at your address. This hyperlink displays your site's primary URL—its home page. Make note of the username, password, and primary URL—all this information is needed when you publish the site.

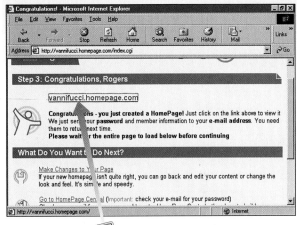

Click

End

How-To Hints

Editing Pages from Your Web Browser

If you have been using FrontPage Express to create a Web site, you can proceed to the next task to learn how to publish it. Alternatively, HomePage.Com enables you to make changes to your Web site directly from your Web browser. To do this, on the page that congratulates you for creating a new HomePage.Com site, click the **Make Changes to Your Page** hyperlink.

Trying Other Free Web Hosting Providers

HomePage.Com is one of the newer free hosting services, so it does not offer some of the features of other sites such as Tripod and Yahoo! GeoCities. Visit the following URLs to try some of the other free hosts:

✓ **Yahoo! GeoCities:** http://geocities.yahoo.com
✓ **Tripod:** http://www.tripod.com
✓ **AcmeCity:** http://www.acmecity.com

7

How to Install the Web Publishing Wizard

Most Web publishing software can be used to transfer the pages and other files of a Web site to a Web server. This process is called *publishing* the site because it makes the site available to the public. FrontPage Express does not have the capability to publish your Web site to a server. You must have software that can transfer files from your computer to the Web server that is hosting your site. Windows includes an optional program that can do this: the Web Publishing Wizard.

Begin

1 Look for the Wizard

To see whether the Web Publishing Wizard is already installed on your computer, right-click any file on your computer. From the context menu that appears, choose **Send To** and look for a **Web Publishing Wizard** command. If you don't see that command (as we don't in the example here), you must install the wizard from the Windows CD.

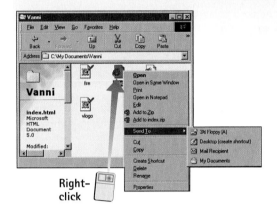

Right-click

2 Open the Control Panel

To begin installing the wizard, place your Windows 98 installation CD in the CD-ROM drive. Click the **Start** button, open the **Settings** folder, and click **Control Panel**. The **Control Panel** window opens.

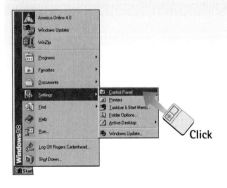

Click

3 Add a Program

Double-click the **Add/Remove Programs** icon. The **Add/Remove Programs Properties** dialog box opens.

Double-click

4 Change Your Windows Setup

Click the **Windows Setup** tab to see what programs are currently installed. Scroll through the list box until you see the **Internet Tools** check box. Place a check mark in this box and click the **Details** button.

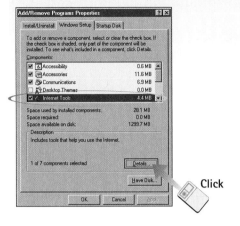

Click

5 Add the Wizard

Check the box next to **Web Publishing Wizard** to select this program to install, then click the **OK** button.

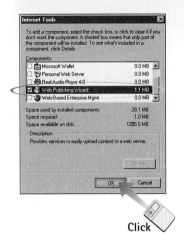

Click

6 Install the Program

Back in the **Add/Remove Programs Properties** dialog box, click the **OK** button to install the Web Publishing Wizard. A **Copying Files** dialog box opens to display the status of the files being copied from the Windows 98 CD to your computer. When the installation is complete, the **Add/Remove Program Properties** dialog box closes.

Click

End

How to Publish Web Pages and Other Files

You can use the Web Publishing Wizard to publish Web pages, images, and anything else stored on your computer. Before you can use the wizard, however, you must know some things about the site that is hosting your files: the username and password you were assigned to use the site and the main URL of your site. If your host requires a type of file transfer called FTP, you also may have to know the FTP server name and your subfolder on that server.

Begin

1 Choose Files to Upload

Open the folder that contains the Web pages, image files, and anything else you want to publish on your Web site. Select the files you want to publish. To select all the files in the folder, choose **Edit, Select All**.

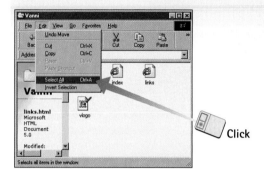

Click

2 Run the Wizard

To publish all the selected files, right-click one of the selected files. From the context menu that appears, choose **Send To** and then choose **Web Publishing Wizard**. The wizard's welcome page opens.

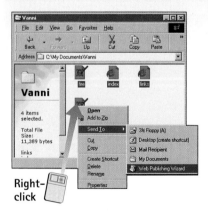

Right-click

3 Name Your Server

The first time you use the wizard, you must set it up to work with a host server. Type the name of your Web host in the **Descriptive name** box and click the **Next** button. This name can be any text that succinctly describes the Web host.

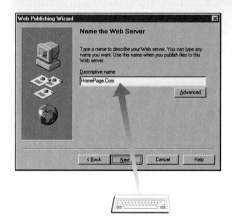

4 Describe Your Site

The **Local directory** text box identifies the folder on your computer where the Web site has been stored. In the **URL** text box, type the primary URL of your Web site—the address a Web user can enter in a browser to visit the site. For HomePage.Com, the URL is the name you picked in Step 2 of Task 6, followed by **.homepage.com** (for example, **http://vannifucci.homepage.com**). Click **Next** to continue.

5 Log In to the Server

You must log in to the Web server that's hosting your site before you can publish files to that server. Type the username and password sent to you by your hosting service in the text boxes provided and click the **OK** button.

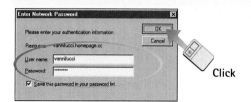

Click

6 Identify Your Provider

Some Web hosts indicate that FTP file transfer is required when you sign up for an account. For HomePage.Com and other hosting services that require FTP, the Web Publishing Wizard may ask you to confirm this information. If your host supports FTP, choose **FTP** from the **Service provider** drop-down list, then click **Next**.

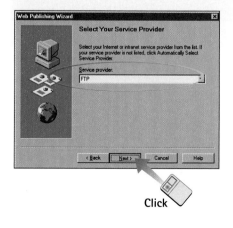

Click

7 Choose Your Server

Fill out the text boxes with information provided by your Web host. HomePage.Com requires you to enter only the primary URL of your site with the **http://** prefix left off (for example, **vannifucci.homepage.com**). Click **Next** to continue. When all questions have been answered, click the **Finish** button to publish your files on the Web. The next time you publish anything on this site, all you need to provide is the site's descriptive name, your username, and your password.

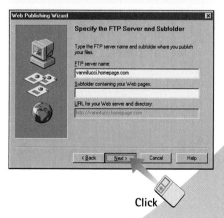

Click

End

Task

14

Using Netscape Navigator to Browse the Web

M ore than 85 percent of all World Wide Web use is conducted on two browsers: Microsoft Internet Explorer and Netscape Navigator.

Navigator is the Web browser included in the Netscape Communicator suite of programs. In the Web's infancy, Navigator was one of the first commercial browsers to be developed, and it remains popular with millions of users today.

Microsoft and Netscape have battled to establish their own browser as the industry leader. Because it is included with Windows and has been frequently updated, Internet Explorer appears to have a large lead in overall use. However, Navigator is certainly comparable to Internet Explorer in terms of features, so the Netscape browser is worth consideration when you're choosing this Internet tool. America Online's purchase of Netscape also means that millions of its users may be encouraged to use Navigator for Web access in the future.

Some Web users routinely keep both leading browsers installed on their computers, and they may even install others, such as Opera. One benefit of installing multiple browsers is your ability to test Web pages you create by loading the pages in each browser to ensure that the widest possible audience can view the documents. ●

How to Download Netscape Navigator

Netscape Navigator is part of Communicator, a suite of programs that also includes email and Usenet capabilities. You can download the current version of the suite from the Netscape Web site. Netscape software can be downloaded using a feature called *SmartDownload*, which enables you to continue an interrupted file transfer where you left off. SmartDownload works by sending a small setup program that you run to download the rest of the files needed for an installation.

Begin

1 Visit Netscape.Com

To visit the Netscape site, launch your current Web browser, type the URL **http://www.netscape.com** in the Address bar, and press **Enter**. The Netscape Netcenter page opens in your browser window.

3 Choose a Program

Click the hyperlink for the version of Netscape Communicator that was designed for your operating system. The download page for that program opens.

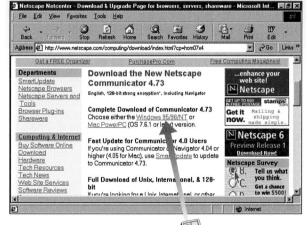

 Click

2 View the Download Page

Click the **Download** hyperlink to view the Communicator download page.

Click

4 Choose a Location

Use the drop-down list to choose the place from which you will download Communicator—the location closest to you is generally the best. Click the **Download** hyperlink to continue.

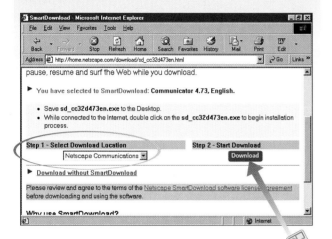

Click

5 Save the Program

Your browser will ask what you want to do with the file that's being downloaded. Click the radio button next to **Save this program to disk**, then click **OK**. The **Save As** dialog box opens.

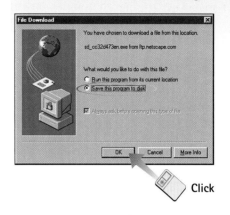

Click

6 Choose a Folder

Use the dialog box to choose a folder on your computer in which you want to save the Communicator suite of programs (a suitable choice is the **My Documents** folder). Then click the **Save** button to store the program in that folder after it is downloaded. You'll see a dialog box indicating the progress of the file transfer as Communicator is downloaded.

Click

7 Complete the Download

After the file has finished downloading, click the **Close** button. Back in your browser, close your Web browser. Now you're ready to install Netscape Communicator, as described in the following task.

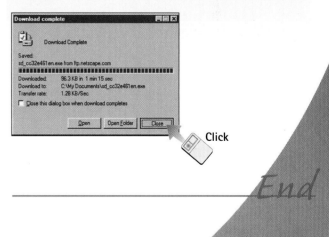

Click

End

How to Install Netscape Navigator

The Netscape Communicator installation program functions like a wizard, asking you simple questions at each step in the process. The most important things to watch for during setup are requests to make Navigator your default Web browser over Internet Explorer 5 or some other browser program. Note that you can use any browser on your computer by running it directly; the default browser runs any time you open a Web page or click a hyperlink in your email program.

Begin

1 Open the Folder

Connect to the Internet and open the folder that contains the setup program you downloaded from Netscape.Com during the previous task. Double-click the program's icon to run it.

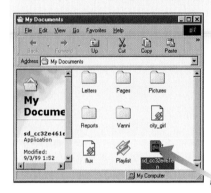

Double-click

2 Install the Program

Remain connected to the Internet but close all other programs on your computer. When that's done, click the **Install** button to begin installing Communicator. The Netscape Communicator Setup window opens and displays the first dialog box in the series.

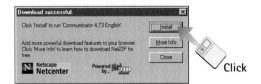

Click

3 Choose a Method

To have more control over whether Communicator takes over some things that were previously handled by Internet Explorer 5, click the **Custom** radio button. Check the **Destination Directory** box to make sure that setup will install Communicator on your hard drive where you want (click the **Browse** button to change the default location) and then click **Next**.

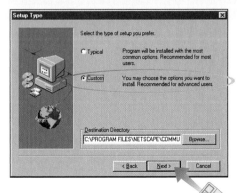

Click

4 Choose Components

Select the boxes next to **Communicator** and any other components you want to install. If you have already installed RealPlayer, deselect that box to avoid overwriting the program. Click **Next** to continue.

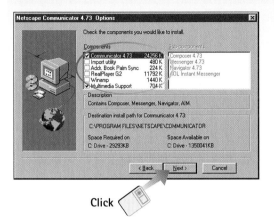

Click

5 Pick Associations

The setup program places check marks next to all the files Navigator will handle. If you want Internet Explorer 5 or some other program to remain the default for all these file types, click **Clear All** to deselect all the boxes. Click **Next** to proceed.

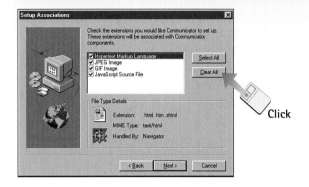

Click

6 Set Up Desktop Options

More check boxes are presented for options Navigator can handle instead of Internet Explorer. Select the boxes for those options you want Navigator to take over. Click **Next** to continue.

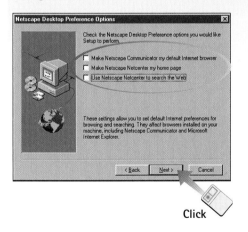

Click

7 Pick a Folder

Specify the folder to which you want the Communicator shortcuts to be added and click **Next**. On the next window that opens, click **Install** to complete the installation of the program.

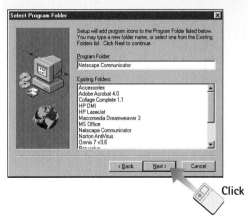

Click

End

How to Set Up Netscape Navigator

When you run Netscape Navigator for the first time, you can create a *user profile* that will store personal browser settings such as your email address, mail server, and Usenet server. Each person who uses Netscape Communicator on your computer can have a different user profile. When you run the browser for the first time, Navigator makes another attempt to become the default Web browser for your computer, if it isn't already.

Begin

1 Run Navigator

To run Netscape Navigator, click the **Start** button, choose **Programs**, **Netscape Communicator**, **Netscape Navigator**. If this is the first time you're running the Navigator browser, the **Enter your Name and Email Address** dialog box opens.

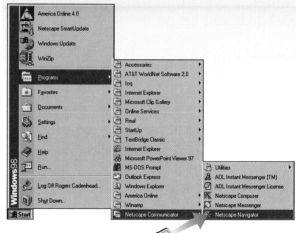

Click

2 Set Up a Profile

Type your name and email address in the text boxes and click **Next**.

3 Name Your Profile

Navigator recommends a name and folder location for your new profile. You can make changes to these recommendations if you want. Click **Next** to continue.

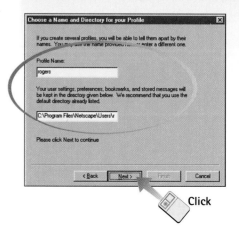

Click

4 Set Your Outgoing Server

Type the name of your Internet service provider's outgoing mail server in the **Outgoing mail (SMTP) server** text box and click **Next**. Most service providers send this information to you when you subscribe; it is often provided on the service provider's Web site as well.

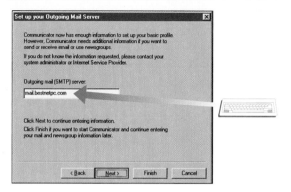

5 Set Your Incoming Server

Type your username and the name of your incoming mail server in the text boxes and click the radio button associated with your server type (usually **POP3**). Click **Next** to continue.

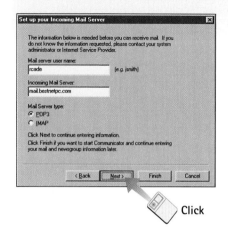

Click

6 Set Your News Server

If you have access to a Usenet server, type its name in the **News (NNTP) server** text box. (Many Internet service providers offer free Usenet access with a subscription—ask your provider for the name of its Usenet server if you can't find it on the company's Web site.) Click **Finish** to create your new user profile with all your settings.

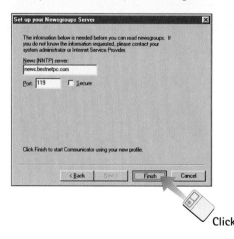

Click

7 Choose a Default

When you run Navigator, the program can detect whether it is the default Web browser on your computer. Click **Yes** if want to make it the default; click **No** otherwise. To prevent this question from being asked again, check the box next to **Do not perform this check in the future**.

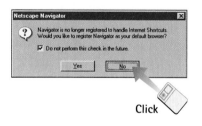

Click

End

How to Revisit Your Favorite Web Pages

If you have already learned how to use Internet Explorer 5, you will pick up the use of another Web browser quickly. Netscape Navigator has most of the same features as Internet Explorer, although some of the names and the menus are different. One feature that has the same name in both browsers is *bookmarks*—shortcuts to your favorite Web sites. You can add a bookmark to a folder of sites you visit often, and you can create folders to organize your bookmarks.

2 Visit a Web Page

To visit a Web page when you know its URL, type the URL in the browser's **Go to** bar and press **Enter**. For this task, go to any Web page for which you want to add a bookmark.

Begin

1 Run Navigator

Before using a browser to visit Web sites, you must connect to the Internet. To run Netscape Navigator, click the **Start** button, choose **Programs**, **Netscape Communicator**, **Netscape Navigator**. If you have more than one Communicator user profile, you'll be asked to pick a profile before the browser runs and opens its home page. Otherwise, the home page loads immediately.

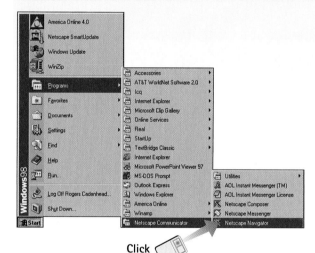

Click

3 Add the Bookmark

To add a bookmark to the Web page that's currently open in your browser, choose **Communicator**, **Bookmarks**, **Add Bookmark**. A bookmark with the page's title is added to Netscape's default **Bookmarks** folder.

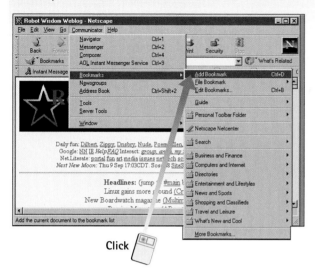

Click

4 File a Bookmark

You also can file a bookmark in a specific folder on your Bookmarks menu. Choose **Communicator**, **Bookmarks**, **File Bookmark**, and then select the folder in which you want to file the bookmark to the current Web page. A bookmark is saved to the indicated folder.

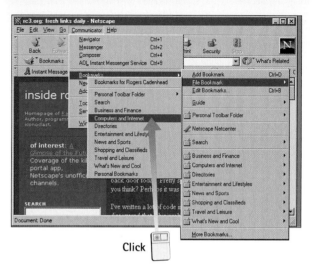

Click

5 Edit Bookmarks

To edit your existing bookmarks, choose **Communicator**, **Bookmarks**, **Edit Bookmarks**. A **Bookmarks** folder opens; you can use it to move, delete, and rename bookmarks.

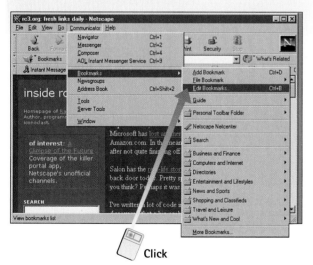

Click

6 Move a Bookmark

To move a bookmark to another folder in the **Bookmarks** window, click the bookmark you want to move, drag it from its current location to the desired folder, and then release the mouse button.

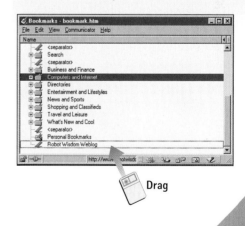

Drag

End

5

How to Change Navigator's Settings

You can configure the performance of Netscape Navigator in several dozen different ways. You can change the browser's home page, which is displayed when you first run the browser and when you click the **Home** icon. You also can determine whether the browser will automatically save *cookies*—information files that help a Web site recognize your identity upon a return visit. Browser settings are called *preferences* in Navigator, and you can change them from the browser's **Edit** menu.

Begin

1 Edit Your Settings

Launch the Netscape Navigator browser. With any Web page displayed, choose **Edit**, **Preferences**. The **Preferences** dialog box opens.

Click

3 Clear History Shortcuts

The browser's **History** folder keeps track of pages you have visited in recent days. After a specified number of days (which you can adjust here), the **History** folder is cleared. If you want to completely empty the **History** folder now, click the **Clear History** button. You may want to empty the **History** folder to maintain your privacy (so that others can't view the sites you've visited) or to regain some disk space.

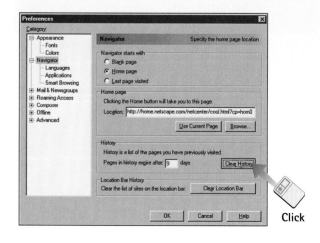

Click

2 Change Your Home Page

To set the browser's home page to the page that's currently displayed in the browser window, click **Navigator** in the **Category** list box, then click the **Use Current Page** button. The **Location** box changes to display the URL of the current page. You can click other **Category** items to view different settings that affect how the browser functions.

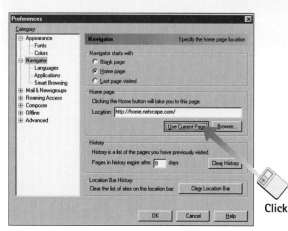

Click

4 Add a Cookie Warning

By default, Navigator accepts all cookies without issuing a warning that it is doing so. To cause the browser to alert you before creating one of these files, click the **Advanced** category in the left pane and check the **Warn me before accepting a cookie** box.

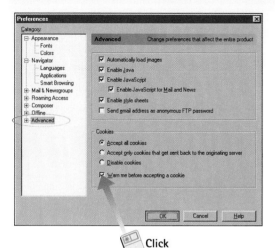

Click

5 Delete Location Shortcuts

Click the **Navigator** category in the left pane to return to the main **Preferences** window. Click the **Clear Location Bar** button to delete all the shortcuts that appear when you click the arrow next to the browser's **Go to** text box.

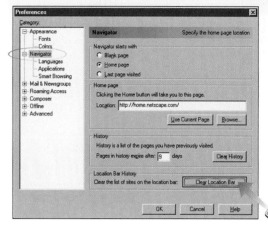

Click

6 Save Your Changes

To close the **Preferences** dialog box and save all your changes, click the **OK** button.

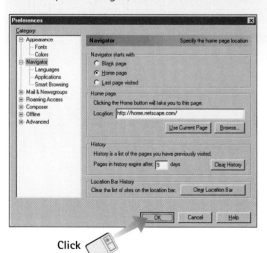

Click

End

How to Find Related Sites

A unique feature of Netscape Navigator is its presentation of sites that are related to the one you're currently viewing. Using World Wide Web traffic data compiled by Alexa Internet, Navigator can present a list of Web sites that appear to be similar to the current site. To compile the list, Navigator compares hyperlinks that connect two sites, patterns of Web use, and other similarities between the sites.

Begin

1 View Site Info

To see information compiled by Alexa about the overall Web site to which the current page belongs, click the **What's Related** button and choose the **Site Info for** menu option. The available information appears in a pop-up box.

Click

2 View a Directory

Netscape shepherds the Open Directory Project, and you can load a relevant page in that directory from the browser. Click the **What's Related** button, choose **Matching Netscape Search Categories**, and click a category.

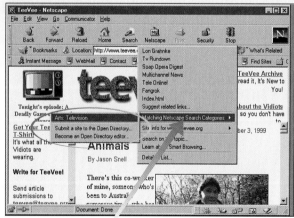

Click

3 See Related Sites

To view all of Navigator's related sites information on a new Web page, click the **What's Related** button and then choose **Detailed List**. The **What's Related Matches** page opens.

Click

4 Visit a Site

Click a hyperlink to visit one of the related sites. Because Alexa continues to collect new World Wide Web usage information, the related sites presented on this page will change over time.

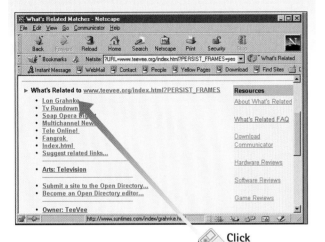

Click

5 Find Out More

The related sites data is one of Navigator's capabilities that Netscape calls *Smart Browsing*. To visit a Web page describing these features, click **What's Related** and then choose **Learn about Smart Browsing**.

Click

End

How-To Hints

Adding Related Sites Capabilities to Internet Explorer 5

Microsoft Internet Explorer 5 does not have a feature that's comparable to Navigator's **What's Related** button. However, the same company that produces the related sites data for Navigator has developed a plug-in that provides similar functionality to Internet Explorer. To download the plug-in, run Internet Explorer and visit the Alexa Web site: type **http://www.alexa.com** in the Address bar and press **Enter**.

Finding Sites in the Open Directory Project

The Open Directory Project is a Web directory compiled by thousands of volunteers and organized into different subject categories. You can use this directory by typing **http://www.dmoz.org** in Navigator's **Netsite** bar and pressing **Enter**. To find out more about using a Web directory like the Open Directory Project, see Part 4, Task 3, "How to Search for a Specific Topic on the Web."

Glossary

A

address book   A personal database of your email correspondents that you can create in Outlook Express. Most other email programs offer a similar feature, including Qualcomm Eudora.

B

bookmarks   Shortcuts to your favorite Web sites. This feature is available in Netscape Navigator, Internet Explorer 5, and other Web browsers. You can add bookmarks to a folder of sites you visit often; you can also create folders to organize your bookmarks.

browser   *See* Web browser.

C

chat room   Also called simply a *chat*. The "place" in cyberspace where people gather to discuss a particular topic. In reality, people sit at their computers, separated by huge distances, and type questions, comments, and criticisms. Other users respond to those comments in real time. Although the discussion may be hampered by slow typing speeds, the effect is that you are sitting in a coffee bar someplace talking over the events of the day with other people who share your interests.

chat   The most immediate way to communicate with someone over the Internet. A chat is a live (real-time), back-and-forth discussion that takes place between two or more people over the Internet instead of over voice telephone lines or in person.

cookie   A special browser file stored on your system that a Web site can use to personalize your visit to the site. Web sites can read the cookie files they have created, which enables a site to recognize who you are when you visit. By design, browsers send cookies only to the site that created them.

D

download   To copy a file from another computer to your system, using a network such as the Internet or another means of connecting computers. You can download data files, programs, and many other types of files from sites all over the Internet to your local server or hard drive. A word of caution: Downloaded files are a major source of computer viruses, so you should have up-to-date antivirus software on any computer to which you are actively downloading files. You also should download files only from sources you know and trust.

E

email (electronic mail) An Internet service that lets you send and receive messages to and from anyone who has an Internet email address. These messages, which are almost always free to send and receive, usually arrive within minutes of being sent.

encryption A way to encode data so that it remains confidential. Some Web servers can encrypt Web pages and other data so that you can enter confidential information on a site, such as when you are buying a product online and want to transmit your credit card information.

F

feedback rating A numeric ranking that is listed with every eBay buyer or seller, so that you can evaluate whether or not you want to do business with that person.

firewall *See* proxy server.

H

handle A screen name that identifies you to the Internet-using public. Comparable to a CB radio handle, an Internet handle can say something about your personality (Grumpy1), your career (BeanCount), or your hobbies (QuiltingB). Of course, it can also be an easy-to-remember moniker such as FirstName.LastName.

heading In FrontPage Express, any text that is formatted in a larger font to serve a similar function to a newspaper headline. FrontPage Express offers six default heading styles that you can use to organize text on your page. Use the Heading1 style for the most important topics on your page; use the remaining styles (Heading2 through Heading6) for subtopics.

home page The first page your browser loads when you start up the browser. Your browser's home page is often a page on the Microsoft Network or one hosted by your computer's manufacturer. There are many *portals* you may want to consider as candidates for your home page. You can specify the home page that loads when you start up the browser. Web sites also have home pages; these pages are the first page you see when you visit a Web site. When you are creating a Web site, the home page is often the one with the filename `index.html`.

host In the context of the World Wide Web, to make pages and other documents (a Web site) available to users of the Internet. Many ISPs provide a limited amount of free space on their servers for you to publish your Web pages; companies are also available that will host sites for free. The provider's server then becomes the host for your site.

hover To position the mouse pointer over an area without clicking the mouse button. Hovering the mouse pointer over a hyperlink on a Web page displays the filename or the URL of the page that will load if you click that hyperlink. Hovering over an area in a program window will frequently display a ScreenTip or a ToolTip.

HTML (HyperText Markup Language) The text markup language used to create Web pages.

hyperlink Text, graphics, or other elements of a Web page that you can click to load a new document into your Web browser. When you click a hyperlink, your browser loads the document to which the link refers; that document can be a Web page, a graphics file, or some other type of information. When you create your own Web page, you can include hyperlinks to any other file—whether that file is a graphics file on your local hard drive or a sound file on somebody else's Web site, for example.

hypertext Text on a Web page you can click to load a new document and jump to a particular location within that document.

I

ICQ The software that pioneered the instant-messaging style of communication. The program is named for the phrase *I Seek You.* An estimated 40 million people have downloaded ICQ's free software, making it the most popular instant-messaging service on the Internet.

instant messaging A style of chat in which you keep track of people you know who are using the same software. A server tells you when selected people are online and provides the same information about you to others. You can send private messages that are received instantly on another user's computer.

Internet service provider (ISP) An ISP offers access to the Internet through your computer's modem. You can find local ISPs in your local Yellow Pages; national ISPs such as America Online, AT&T WorldNet, and CompuServe are also options. All ISPs offer assistance in setting up your computer to work with the Internet.

M

mailing list A group discussion that takes place entirely with email. People who are interested in a list's topic send an email message to a specific address to subscribe. If the list allows public participation (as many do), you can use a special email address to send a message to all members. Any message sent by another member to the list of subscribers appears in your Inbox.

MP3 (MPEG-1 Audio Layer 3) A popular format for presenting recorded sound on a computer. The format was developed with the goal of preserving sound quality while making files as small as possible.

N

netiquette Commonly accepted standards for behavior on the Internet.

news server An Internet site that can send and receive Usenet newsgroup messages.

news In the context of Usenet, public messages contributed to the newsgroup.

newsgroups *See* Usenet.

O

offline viewing Looking at a Web document while not actually connected to the Internet. If your telephone and your computer share the same line, you can look at pages offline as you're talking on the phone—which you can't do if you're viewing online.

P

portal A commercial Web site that functions as a gateway to the Internet. If you designate a portal as your browser's home page, you can start every online session on that page, giving some structure to your Internet experience.

proxy server A server set up between your computer and the Internet (generally in an office or academic environment). To get to the Internet, you have to go through the proxy server, which performs security checks to make sure that outsiders cannot access your company's network illegally. Also called a *firewall.*

publish To upload files to a Web server to make those files available to users of the Internet. Although you can create wonderful Web pages using FrontPage Express, those pages cannot be viewed by users of the Internet until they are published to a Web server that has direct access to the Internet.

S

ScreenTip   A small pop-up box containing text that defines or describes a particular area of the screen. You can display a ScreenTip by hovering the mouse cursor over the area of the screen in question. Some applications call the ScreenTips that appear for toolbar buttons *ToolTips*.

search engines   World Wide Web sites that use computers to catalog millions of Web pages, which you can use to search for specific text. Some of the most popular search engines are AltaVista (`http://www.altavista.com`), Google (`http://www.google.com`), MetaCrawler (`http://www.metacrawler.com`), and HotBot (`http://www.hotbot.com`).

secure Web server   Most often used for online shopping. A secure server encrypts information (such as a credit card number) that is sent to the server and received from it so that confidential information is hidden from anyone who might try to view it.

security certificate   A special browser window that vouches for the authenticity of a program's author. After you see the security certificate, you can decide whether you want to let the program run on your machine. A security certificate is required only when you're working with ActiveX technology; Java doesn't require this kind of direct action by the user.

server   A computer that sends information to other computers, either in response to a request or through an automated schedule. A popular type of server on the Internet is a Web server.

signature file   Text that is automatically appended to email, Usenet postings, and similar documents. These files often contain your name, email address, favorite quote, and other personal information.

SmartDownload   A Netscape Communicator feature that enables you to continue an interrupted file transfer where you left off. SmartDownload works by sending a small setup program that you run to download the rest of the files needed for an installation.

spam   A kind of unsolicited Internet marketing in which thousands of email messages are sent out to anyone with an email account. An electronic version of junk mail, spam often promotes unsavory businesses and is forged so that the sender's identity is hidden. Spam is a widely loathed practice that is illegal to send in a few jurisdictions. The name was inspired by a Monty Python comedy sketch and is unrelated to the Hormel spiced meat product of the same name.

status area   The part of your Windows taskbar that's next to the current time (usually in the lower-right corner of the display screen). This is also called the *system tray*, and it may contain icons representing your Internet connection, speaker volume, antivirus software, and other programs that are running on your computer.

streaming audio   Sound on the Internet that begins playing as soon as the file is selected rather than at the end of a complete download of the sound file. This format is especially well suited for concerts and live radio.

synchronization   In Outlook Express, the process of receiving new messages in Usenet newsgroups you have subscribed to.

system tray   *See* status area.

T

taskbar   The strip along the bottom or side of your Windows display screen in which appear the Start button, the buttons for all active programs, the current system time, and the status area.

ticker symbol   A short, unique code assigned to a company by the stock exchange on which that company trades.

ToolTip   *See* ScreenTip.

U

URL (uniform resource locator)   A unique address that identifies a document on the World Wide Web. You can direct your browser to a particular Web page by typing the page's URL in an address field and pressing Enter. A site's address can take many forms, but most of the largest Web sites have similar-looking and simple URLs, such as `http://www.yahoo.com`, `http://www.mcp.com`, and `http://www.theobvious.com`.

Usenet   A collection of public discussion groups covering a diverse range of topics. Usenet groups, which also are called *newsgroups*, are distributed by thousands of Internet sites around the world.

W

Web browser   The tool that lets you view pages on the World Wide Web. After you connect to the Internet, you load a browser; then you can see and interact with pages on the Web. Some of the most popular browsers are Microsoft Internet Explorer and Netscape Navigator. Internet Explorer 5 is used in many of the tasks in this book.

Web directory   World Wide Web sites that use human editors to categorize thousands of Web sites according to their content and make recommendations about the best sites. The main way to use these directories is to navigate to the categories you are interested in. Web directories include Yahoo! (`http://www.yahoo.com`), Lycos (`http://www.lycos.com`), Infoseek (`http://www.infoseek.com`), and the Open Directory Project (`http://www.dmoz.org`).

Web server   A server on the Internet that sends Web pages and other documents in response to requests by Web browsers. Everything you view on the World Wide Web is delivered by a Web server to your browser. *See also* server.

Web site   A group of related Web pages. When you are creating Web pages in a program such as FrontPage Express, you should make an effort to link all the pages together as a site.

Index

content ratings, setting (IE), 70-71

Control Panel, opening, 180

cookies, 44
  disabling, 74-75
  warnings (Netscape Navigator), 207

Create Hyperlink dialog box, 185

Create Screen Names link (AOL), 140

creating
  email messages, 80
  ICQ accounts, 120-121
  new chat rooms (AOL), 137
  newsgroup accounts, 101
  Outlook Express accounts, 78-79
  signature files (newsgroups), 112-113

Ctrl+I keyboard shortcut, 138

Ctrl+M keyboard shortcut, 132

Customize Settings button, 141

customizing
  portals, 44
  security settings, 68-69

D

default directories, selecting, 131

Deja.Com, 109-111

deleting
  email messages, 82
  Favorites list sites, 27

History list items, 53
users from ICQ contact lists, 123

descriptions of newsgroups, 108

desktop, Online Services folder, 130

Dial-Up Networking folder, 10

dialog boxes
  Add/Remove Programs Properties, 180
  Confirmation, 133
  Connect To, 9
  Connected, 9, 11
  Create Hyperlink, 185
  File Download, 59
  Installing, 131
  Internet Options, 12, 25, 32-33
  Internet Tools, 180
  Make New Connection, 8
  Print, 34
  Save As, 17
  Windows Update, 18

digital certificates (security), 72-73

directories, 49, 54
  category pages, 55
  newsgroups, 109
  selecting, default, 131

disconnecting, 9, 11

discussion groups. See newsgroups

disks, AOL, installing, 131

displaying newsgroups, 102-104

dithering graphics, 97

documents as home pages, 31

Download Now button, 16

Download.com, 58-59, 116

downloading
  AOL, 130-131
  ICQ, 116-117
  Internet Explorer 5, 16-19
  MP3
    players, 144-145
    songs, 147
  Netscape Navigator, 198-199
  newsgroups, 101, 105
  RealPlayer, 150-151
  SmartDownload, 198-199
  software, 58-59
  Windows Media Player, 154

Drudge, Matt, 179

E

EBay Web site, 162-165

.edu URL suffix, 51

electronic mail. See email

electronic mailing lists. See mailing lists

email. See also chatting; Outlook Express
  addresses, 62-63, 79, 88-89
    Internet, 133
    linking to, 187
  AOL, 132-133
  carbon copies, 132
  composing, 132-133
  Confirmation dialog box, 133
  dithering graphics, 97
  HTML format, 80-81
  hyperlinks, 36
  incoming mail servers, 78
  junk mail, redirecting, 95
  mailing lists, 90-91